D0576678

# MAN AND
# BEAST

## QUEST FOR THE UNKNOWN

# MAN AND BEAST

Reader's Digest

**THE READER'S DIGEST ASSOCIATION, INC.**
Pleasantville, New York/Montreal

Quest for the Unknown
Created, edited, and designed by DK Direct Limited

# A DORLING KINDERSLEY BOOK

Copyright © 1993 The Reader's Digest Association, Inc.
Copyright © 1993 The Reader's Digest Association (Canada) Ltd.
Copyright © 1993 Reader's Digest Association Far East Ltd.
Philippine Copyright 1993 Reader's Digest Association Far East Ltd.

All rights reserved. Unauthorized reproduction, in any manner, is prohibited.

## DK DIRECT LIMITED

**Series Editor** Richard Williams
**Editors** Deirdre Headon, Tony Whitehorn
**Editorial Research** Julie Whitaker

**Senior Art Editor** Susie Breen
**Art Editor** Mark Osborne
**Designer** Juliette Norsworthy
**Senior Picture Researcher** Frances Vargo
**Picture Researcher** Lesley Coleman; **Picture Assistant** Sharon Southren

**Editorial Director** Jonathan Reed; **Design Director** Ed Day
**Production Manager** Ian Paton

**Volume Consultant** Dr. Karl P. N. Shuker
**Commissioning Editor** Peter Brookesmith
**Contributors** Benedict Allen, Janet Bord, Mark Chorvinsky, Loren Coleman, Peter Costello,
Hilary Evans, Michael Goss, J. Richard Greenwell, Mark A. Hall, David Heppell, Nicholas Jones,
Robert Kiener, Prof. Grover S. Krantz, Dr. Roy P. Mackal, Dr. Myra Shackley, Dr. Karl P. N. Shuker

**Illustrators** Jonathan Bentley, Roy Flooks, Emma Parker, Clive Pritchard, Matthew Richardson
**Photographers** Zafer Baran, Simon Farnhell, Andrew Griffin, Mark Hamilton, Gary Marsh,
Steve Rawlings, Paul Venning, Alex Wilson

### Library of Congress Cataloging in Publication Data

Man and beast.
          p.     cm. — (Quest for the unknown)
      "A Dorling Kindersley book."
      Includes index.
      ISBN 0-89577-496-8
      1. Animals, Mythical.  2. Monsters.   3. Animals—Folklore.
      I. Reader's Digest Association.   II. Series.
      GR825.M19 1993
      398'.369—dc20                                        92-47142

READER'S DIGEST and the Pegasus logo are registered trademarks of
The Reader's Digest Association, Inc.

Printed in the United States of America

# FOREWORD

*D*EPENDING ON ANIMALS FOR FOOD and fur for warmth, primitive man knew that his destiny was linked with that of the beasts. His almost religious fascination with the creatures he hunted is evidenced by cave drawings found as far apart as France and Australia. Many early civilizations revered animals as the incarnation of gods; in ancient Egypt, for example, both the cobra and the cat were objects of worship.

Another kind of transformation, in which humans turn into beasts, has become deeply ingrained in the popular imagination. Often such metamorphoses are associated with fear and terror. In central and eastern Europe, for example, a belief in the bloodsucking vampire that condemns its victims to a living death has persisted into the 20th century. And in West Africa until recently, members of a secret society called the Leopard Men believed that simply wearing the leopard's distinctive spotted skin would magically imbue them with that animal's fearsome strength.

We are all familiar with such legendary creatures as the Loch Ness monster, Bigfoot, and the Yeti. During the last 30 years, however, a branch of zoology has grown up that focuses on the possibility that such astonishing creatures may actually exist. This study, which is called cryptozoology (meaning the science of hidden animals), has astounded many skeptical observers with its controversial but cogent arguments that such creatures might be descendants of animals long believed to be extinct.

This volume describes and explains the extent of humankind's extraordinary fascination with the animal kingdom. Despite the advances of modern science, however, you will not find all the answers in these pages. The reason: Many mysteries remain to be unraveled.

*— The Editors*

# CONTENTS

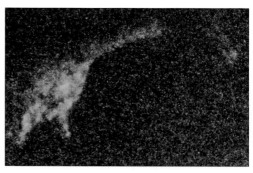

# THE WILDMAN OF CHINA

*For the past 2,000 years there have been reports of a mysterious creature, half-human, half-ape, living in the remote forests of central China. Could this bizarre animal be real — or is it simply an imaginary beast created out of man's fascination with the unknown?*

The jeep's headlights picked out the lonely, winding country road ahead. All else was impenetrable darkness, the night's oppressiveness deepened by the brooding presence of primeval forest rearing up to the sky.

It was 1:00 A.M. on May 14, 1976, and the jeep's passengers — five Chinese forestry officials — were returning home from a conference. In the stillness of the night they were aware of the vastness of the

## LAUGHING KILLER

*According to a Chinese folktale about Wildman, the creature eats people. Coming across a human, it grips his or her arms tightly, making escape impossible. It is apparently so overjoyed by trapping its prey that it faints with mirth — but without loosening its hold. When it returns to its senses, it kills and eats its victim.*

*Thus travelers in the mountains were advised to wear a pair of hollow bamboo cylinders on their arms. If a Wildman caught them, they could then, while the creature was in a swoon, slip their arms out of the cylinders and escape.*

## MOUNTAIN ATTACK

*In 1981 Gong Yulan, a peasant woman of Hubei province, claimed that five years earlier, while cutting pig fodder on a mountain slope, she saw an animal with reddish-black hair scratching itself against a tree. According to Gong's story, when the creature saw her and her four-year-old son, it charged them. She picked up her child and fled down the mountain until she reached safety. Gong said that the animal rubbed itself against the tree in the way a human would and that it also moved like a man.*

forest reserve of Shennongjia — still only partially explored — all around them. It contained great trees whose roots trailed back millions of years, and in it, too, there allegedly lived a strange half-human, half-ape, known as the Yeren, or Wildman....

The jeep passed through the sleeping village of Chunshuya. Suddenly, the headlights picked out a strange creature, some way ahead and just beside the

> ### The creature stared into the headlights.... The brown face was apelike, with a protruding snout and large ears — yet the eyes were like a human's.

road. The driver switched the headlights to high beam, sounded the horn, and drove rapidly toward the beast. Alarmed, the creature tried to climb the cliff beside the road. Some way up, however, it slipped down and fell into the road, where the approaching jeep screeched to a halt to avoid running over it.

### Humanlike eyes

On all fours, its large hindquarters raised high, the creature stared into the headlights. While the driver continued to sound the horn, the five forestry workers jumped out of the jeep and approached the animal. A bizarre sight met their eyes. The creature appeared to be five to six feet tall and was covered in soft, thin, reddish-brown hair, with a lock of deep purplish-red hair on its back. The brown face was apelike, with a protruding snout and large ears — yet the eyes were like a human's. Belly and buttocks were plump, arms and legs long and thick. The creature had no tail. It moved slowly, clumsily, and soundlessly.

One of the startled onlookers, Shu Jiaguo, vice-chairman of the regional forestry committee, said later: "I have been a hunter since I was a boy and have seen all kinds of animals, but I have never seen a red-haired creature like this. No one dared to touch it."

Eventually, Zhou Zhongyi, chief of the agricultural bureau, threw a stone at the animal, hitting it on the buttocks. It stood up on its hind legs, slowly walked down a ditch at the roadside, mounted a slope, and disappeared into the forest. The Wildman of Shennongjia had apparently returned to the obscurity from which it had so briefly and tantalizingly emerged....

## SHOOTING BY THE ROADSIDE

Several decades earlier, in 1940, Wang Zelin, a biologist working for the Yellow River Irrigation Committee, was traveling on a bus when he and the other passengers heard gunshots ahead. "Soon the firing stopped, and in a quarter of an hour we reached the scene and saw a crowd on the road ahead. We reached them and asked what they were doing there.

"'We are hunters of the Wildman,' they replied....'Here it is. We are going to haul it to the county government to see what should be done with it.'

"Our curiosity aroused, we got off the bus and took a look. After all these years, I still remember every detail.

### Body still warm

"Lying by the side of the road was the Wildman, still supple because it had just been killed. I thought the body was still warm, though I didn't touch it. It was more than six feet tall and covered with a dense coat of grayish-red hair about one inch long. It lay face down. A curious onlooker, one of my fellow-passengers, turned it over, and we saw it was a female....The large teats were red, suggesting a baby had just been born and was being breast-fed....

"Its head looked not much bigger than a human's, but the Wildman's face was overgrown with hair which was shorter than that on the rest of the body....The cheekbones were high, the eyes deep-set. Its jaws were protruding.... The appearance of the head was similar to that of the plaster model of Peking Man [an early form of man dating from

> "Lying by the side of the road was the Wildman, still supple because it had just been killed.... It was more than six feet tall and covered with a dense coat of grayish-red hair about one inch long...we saw it was a female...."

300,000–500,000 years ago], but the hair seemed longer and thicker. The shoulders were broad...the hands were very big with long fingers and fingernails. The feet were more than a foot long....

### Very powerful

"Local inhabitants told us that two Wildmen, probably a mating pair, had appeared in the neighborhood and been there for over a month. They said that the Wildmen were very powerful, stood upright, and moved swiftly. They climbed mountains without difficulty, and it was impossible to overtake them. They had no language, but simply uttered cries."

Wang continued on his journey. There is no record of what happened to the corpse of the alleged Wildman.

## "EMACIATED OLD MAN"

*In August 1977 Xiao Xingyang, a young forestry worker, was in the forest in the Shennongjia region when, he claimed, he saw a strange creature emerge from the trees. He described it as being about five feet high and standing on its hind legs. It was covered in long, dark brown hair but otherwise looked just like a human being. The face, he said, had sunken eyes, an upturned nose, and buck teeth, and resembled that of an emaciated old man. He was so frightened, he claimed, that he ran away immediately.*

*Two of Xiao's companions later reported that, as their pale and breathless friend was telling them his story, they heard a strange two-note cry in the direction Xiao had come from: the first note was husky, the second shrill.*

## HORRIFYING "HAIRY MAN"

*In October 1976 He Qicui, a schoolteacher of Hubei province, was picking wild fruit with a group of pupils in the countryside when, she claimed, they saw a yellowish-red "hairy man" walking upright up a hillside. Some of the pupils ran away in terror, others stayed with their teacher until the creature disappeared out of sight over the hill.*

## SLOW PURSUIT

*In May 1981 Ye Wan Chou and Chen Zong Chun, two eight-year-old children of Sichuan province, were tending sheep when, they said, they saw a large, red-haired, manlike animal in a squatting position. Scared, they ran off, but the creature followed them for a while. It moved slowly, they claimed, and on its hind legs, like a man.*

## MEETING IN THE FOREST

Another remarkable account of an alleged meeting with Wildman was given in 1977 by commune team leader Pang Gensheng, of Shaanxi province. In early June of that year he was cutting wood in a forest gully on a mountainside, when he came across a "hairy man." Pang recounted what happened next:

### Cornered by a Wildman

"It came closer and closer. I got scared and kept retreating until my back was against a stone cliff and I couldn't go any farther. The hairy man came to within seven or eight feet, and then to a distance of five feet. I raised my ax, ready to fight for my life. We stood like that, neither of us moving...."

Pang described the creature in this way: "He was about seven feet tall, with shoulders wider than a man's, a sloping forehead, deep-set eyes, and a bulbous nose with slightly flared nostrils. He had sunken cheeks, ears like a man's but larger, and round eyes, also bigger than a man's. His jaw jutted out and he had protruding lips. His front teeth were as broad as a horse's. His eyes were black. His hair was dark brown and more than a foot long, and hung loosely over his shoulders. His face, except for the nose and ears, was covered with short hair.

### Big hands

"His arms hung down below his knees. He had big hands with fingers about six inches long and with thumbs only slightly separated from the fingers. He didn't have a tail and the hair on his body was short. He had thick thighs, shorter than his calves. He walked upright, with his legs apart. His feet were about a foot long and half that width, with splayed toes."

### Howled several times

According to Pang, the two stood facing each other for more than an hour. "Then I groped for a stone," said Pang, "and threw it at him. It hit him in the chest. He howled several times and rubbed the spot with his left hand. After that he moved off to the left and leaned against a tree, then walked away slowly toward the bottom of the gully."

"I kept retreating until my back was against a stone cliff and I couldn't go any farther. The hairy man came to within seven or eight feet, and then to a distance of five feet. I raised my ax, ready to fight for my life."

## COMMENT

The belief that a strange half-human, half-ape creature inhabits the dense forests of central China is not a new one. Such stories, in fact, date back more than 2,000 years. References to creatures of this type recur in Chinese literature, and many sightings have been reported, particularly in the past few decades.

But what are the chances that Wildman actually exists?

In the 1950's Chinese scientists decided to investigate the matter, and since then they have mounted several expeditions into the areas where the creature is supposed to live.

### Hair analysis

Among other things, the scientists collected more than 100 so-called Wildman hairs. Analyzing them with PIXE (particle-induced X-ray emission), they apparently found that there was 50 times more iron and zinc in the hairs than in human hairs, and 7 times more than in primate hairs. This is an intriguing finding, yet one that needs to be further interpreted.

The results from investigating more than 1,000 "Wildman footprints," however, have been disappointing. The footprints vary enormously in size, and most are indistinct. Some might easily have been made by humans and the others by apes or monkeys.

Examination of feces allegedly produced by Wildmen has shown only that they probably came from some kind of omnivorous primate. And scientists are doubtful about the authenticity of Wildman nests — beds of foliage apparently made by pulling seven or so bamboo trees together — because of the tremendous strength that would be required to accomplish this.

Apart from reported sightings, such inconclusive evidence is all that there is to support the possible existence of Wildmen. No remains of one have ever been examined by scientists, and no photograph of one has ever been taken.

It is not surprising, therefore, that most scientists believe that reported sightings of the creature are, when not actually hoaxes, most likely to be mis-sightings of known animals, such as golden monkeys, bears, or orangutans. Some scientists, however, believe that the Wildman case remains open, that it is possible that creatures as yet unknown to science might exist in remote areas of the world. The most popular theory among these

> ## Some scientists believe that creatures as yet unknown might exist in remote areas of the world.

scientists is that Wildman might be a surviving form of *Gigantopithecus*, a large ape that existed for 8 million years and supposedly became extinct 300,000–500,000 years ago. They emphasize that other animals living at the time of *Gigantopithecus*, such as the giant panda, Malaysian tapir, and orangutan, have survived to the present day — and the giant panda escaped detection by science until 1869.

### Continuing speculation

That *Gigantopithecus* might have survived is, however, pure speculation. Anthropologist Dr. Frank E. Poirier, of Ohio State University, wonders in fact if Wildman may not simply be a figment of the imagination. He asks: "Do humans have a 'need' to believe in the existence of such mysterious creatures?"

**Sources:** *Articles by J. Richard Greenwell, Frank E. Poirier, Hu Hongxing, Chung-Min Chen, and Zhou Guoxing, published in* Cryptozoology *magazine. Additional information supplied by Loren Coleman.*

## "MONKEY BABIES"

*Some of those searching for Wildman have suggested that the "monkey babies" allegedly born in some rural areas of central China could be the result of matings between Wildmen and humans. These infants are said to have a small, strangely shaped head, to be covered in hair from head to toe, and to have a low intelligence and no speech.*

*However, anthropologist Dr. Frank E. Poirier, of Ohio State University, among others, has declared that it is genetically impossible for a nonhuman primate and a human to produce progeny. And Dr. Zhou Guoxing, of the Beijing Natural History Museum, who examined the skeleton of a so-called monkey baby, concluded that it was simply the remains of a deformed human child.*

## SEVERED HANDS

*In May 1957 it was reported that a Wildman, with a humanlike face, had been beaten to death on a mountainside in Zhejiang province. A schoolteacher took possession of, and preserved, the hands and feet that were said to have been severed from the animal. In 1980 Dr. Zhou Guoxing examined these specimens and concluded that they might have come from an "enormous monkey," perhaps a previously unrecorded species of macaque.*

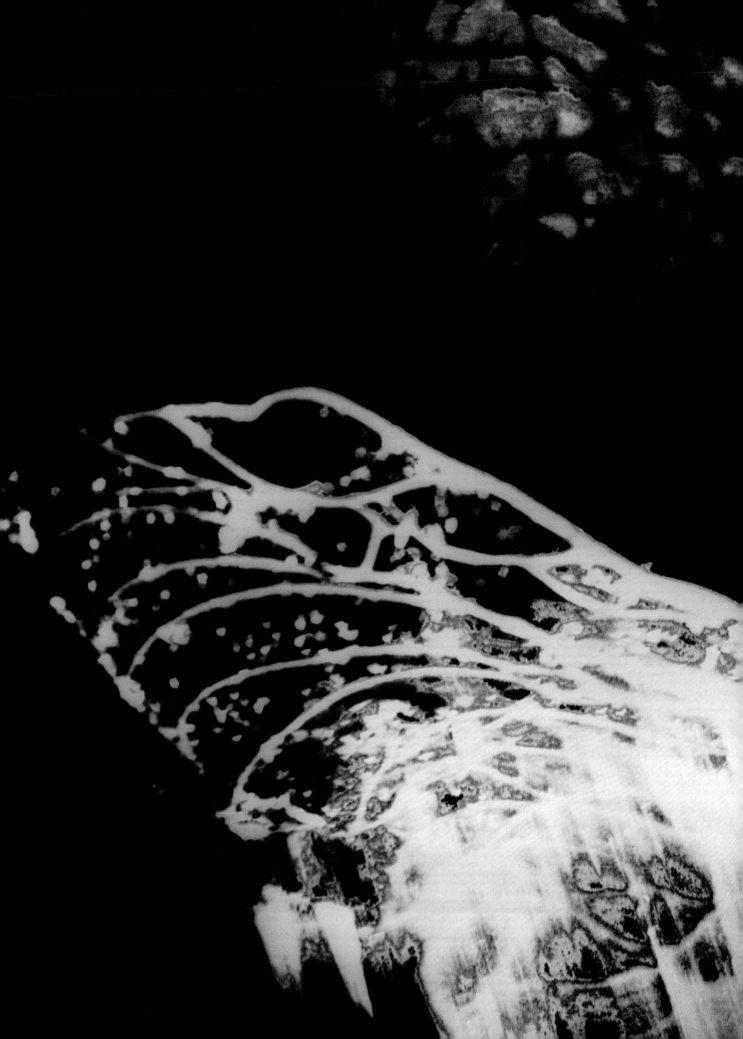

# CHAPTER ONE

# MONSTERS ON THE WING

*Giant birdmen, flying jackals, a batwoman, cats with wings — there have been many reports from around the world of astonishing flying creatures. Often seen at night, these creatures are sometimes described by frightened eye-witnesses as flying monsters.*

Late on the night of November 15, 1966, Mr. and Mrs. Roger Scarberry were driving with their friends, Mr. and Mrs. Steve Mallette, through a disused Second World War ammunition dump, known locally as the TNT Area, in Point Pleasant, West Virginia. As they passed an abandoned generator building, they suddenly caught sight of a pair of red disks that resembled eyes glowing in the dark. Peering intently, they were astonished to see a gray figure, bigger than a man. In place of arms, it appeared

**Gray monster**
*An eyewitness's impression of Mothman.*

to have large wings, which were folded against its back. This strange creature, part bird, part man, was shuffling along the ground.

Roger Scarberry immediately pressed down hard on the accelerator, but to his horror the creature opened its wings, took off, and flew above the speeding automobile, keeping pace with the vehicle, even though Scarberry later claimed that he reached a speed of 100 m.p.h. The bird disappeared once they left the TNT Area. They went to the sheriff's office to report the incident, but a search of the ammunition dump revealed no trace of the strange creature.

### Glowing red eyes
The next day Mrs. Marcella Bennett was visiting friends who lived close to the TNT Area. As Mrs. Bennett left her car, carrying her infant daughter, she claimed she saw the same gray creature with glowing red eyes suddenly loom up before her. Mrs. Bennett was so startled that she dropped her baby. Quickly picking up her child, she ran to her

---

## The creature made its way with a shuffling gait onto the porch and peered in the window.

---

friends' house, gained entry, and locked the door behind her. The creature made its way with a shuffling gait onto the porch and peered in the window.

### Mothman
The winged creature became known as Mothman. During the next 13 months Mothman plagued the Point Pleasant area of West Virginia. Writer John Keel, in his book *The Mothman Prophecies* (1975), interviewed over a hundred people who had seen the winged monster first-hand. From their accounts, he was able to build up a detailed picture of Mothman.

The creature was described as being between five and seven feet tall. It did not have arms but wings like those of a bat that were folded against its back when not in use; its legs were like those of a man; it had shoulders but no neck; its eyes were red and two to three inches wide, and set near to the top of its shoulders. Witnesses estimated its wingspan at about 10 feet. Thirteen months after the first sighting Mothman vanished as suddenly as it had appeared.

### Aggressive bird
Various theories have been put forward to explain the mysterious birdman. Dr. Robert Smith, of the biology department of West Virginia University, has suggested that it might well have been a rare sandhill crane. This large gray bird, with a bald red forehead, has the reputation of being an aggressive bird that might

**Churchyard owl**
*The Cornish Owlman was seen near the village church in Mawnan, England (right). Ornithologists have suggested that the giant owl might have been an escaped eagle owl (top right).*

### CRYPTOZOOLOGY
The eminent French zoologist Dr. Bernard Heuvelmans first coined the term cryptozoology (meaning the science of hidden animals). This field of study includes investigating out-of-place animals, mysterious animals, and supposedly extinct creatures.

Heuvelmans believes that certain species might have survived in obscurity from ancient times. He has suggested that certain wildernesses — such as parts of America and Africa — might conceal unknown creatures.

### Animals awaiting discovery
Heuvelmans has written a series of meticulously researched books, of which *Sur la Piste des Bêtes Ignorées (On the Track of Unknown Animals)* (1955) was the first. In this book Heuvelmans concluded that there were at least 30 species of large land animals still unknown to science, or long thought to be extinct, that might be awaiting discovery.

This book was very popular with general readers, and introduced cryptozoology to a wider audience.

well run or even fly after people. And since the sandhill crane is not native to West Virginia, its appearance there would be unlikely and unexpected and might well cause alarm. It is also possible that the West Virginia sightings were of a giant stork.

## Extraterrestrial life

So strange did Mothman appear to people that when reports of the sightings spread, some paranormal researchers suggested that it came from outer space, or even from another dimension of reality. John Keel pointed out that unidentified flying objects (UFO's) had been sighted in the Point Pleasant area in the 1960's, and that there was a similarity between the experience of seeing Mothman, or other creatures, and the experience of seeing a flying saucer.

Mark Hall, who has investigated the numerous sightings of mysterious big birds in America, has argued that the description of Mothman corresponds with reports of another strange bird known as Bighoot, a giant owl

with a wingspan estimated at 10 feet. Bighoot is also described as a gray bird with glowing red eyes.

Giant owls figure in the lore of American Indians, whose legends tell of a creature called the Great Owl. Folktales of the early European settlers refer to a similar creature, which was called the Booger-Owl. These owls have been reported in the Allegheny Plateau in Pennsylvania, the Ozark Mountains in Missouri, and the Pacific Northwest. However, no bones as yet have been discovered to support the existence of such a formidable owl.

## Cornish Owlman

Sightings of mysterious giant owls are not restricted to North America. In 1976 there was a series of reports of a giant owlman in the vicinity of the church in the village of Mawnan, in Cornwall, in the southwest of England. On the evening of April 17, 1976, a giant owl was reportedly seen hovering around the church tower by two young girls. On July 3, 1976, two other young girls said they encountered the same bird. Sally Chapman, age 14, was camping with a friend in some woods near the church. As she stood outside her tent, she heard a hissing sound, and turned to see a figure standing a short distance away among the pine trees.

## Pincer-like claws

According to Sally, this figure looked like an owl as big as a man, covered with gray feathers, with pointed ears and glowing red eyes. When Sally and her friend, Barbara Perry, burst out laughing at the sight of the creature, believing it was somebody in fancy dress, the Owlman flew up into the air, revealing black pincer-like claws. The Cornish Owlman, as it became known, was seen by other witnesses the next day and on one occasion two years later, in 1978. All the sightings centered on Mawnan church.

In *Alien Animals* (1985) British paranormal researchers Janet and Colin Bord point out that Mawnan church is built in the middle of a prehistoric earthwork. They suggest that the church may be

**BIRD OF DOOM**

On Culloden Moor in the Scottish Highlands, on the evening of April 15, 1746, Highland soldiers reportedly saw a winged monster flying over their lines as they waited on the eve of battle.

They had supposedly seen the Skree, a bird with a human head, burning red eyes, and black leathery wings. As it hovered over the soldiers, the bird, as the Highland general Lord George Murray later reported, emitted a chilling scream. The soldiers were terror-struck because, according to Highland folklore, to see the Skree presaged misfortune.

### Day of battle

The morning after the sighting of the Skree the Battle of Culloden took place. This battle lasted a mere 40 minutes, and was the bloodiest in British history. Thousands of Highlanders were slain by the English soldiers. No mercy was shown to those who survived the battle. They were pursued and slaughtered.

***Owl of creation***
*Giant owls appear in many American Indian tales. This earthenware owl-shaped vessel was made by the Pueblo Indians of New Mexico.*

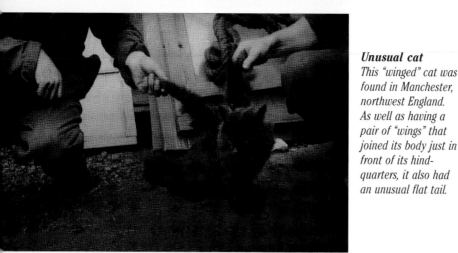

*Unusual cat*
*This "winged" cat was found in Manchester, northwest England. As well as having a pair of "wings" that joined its body just in front of its hindquarters, it also had an unusual flat tail.*

## CATS WITH WINGS

On June 10, 1933, a London newspaper, the *Sunday Dispatch*, published a photograph of a black and white cat with an impressive pair of wings that joined its body just in front of its hindquarters. It could supposedly move them up and down. The cat, which was exhibited at Oxford Zoo, allegedly used its wings to enable it to leap considerable distances.

### Canadian flying cat

Over the years, winged cats have been reported around the world. In Alfred, Ontario, Canada, in 1966, eyewitnesses reported a fanged black cat that could actually fly. This creature was shot on June 24 by a local storekeeper, when it attempted to attack another cat. Examination of the carcass proved its wings to be merely matted clumps of fur.

### Skin disorder

English zoologist Dr. Karl P. N. Shuker, however, believes he has solved the mystery of flying cats. He discovered scientific papers on a very obscure, genetically inherited skin disorder of cats, called feline cutaneous asthenia (F.C.A.). Cats displaying F.C.A. have abnormally fragile skin that is remarkably elastic in nature, readily stretching to form furry winglike extensions along the back and elsewhere.

built on a ley line (a straight line that passes through and links several ancient sites), and speculate that the appearance of the Owlman may be a manifestation of earth energy in this place.

A more reasonable explanation may be that the Owlman sightings were of an escaped eagle owl, a species that can grow more than two feet long, with a wingspan of nearly six feet.

### Bahamian birdman

Sometimes it is claimed physical traces of giant winged creatures have been found. In the forests and swamps of Andros, the largest island in the Bahamas chain, extraordinary nests have been discovered which local folklore says were built by a giant birdman called the Chick-charney. The nests have been constructed in a very distinctive way. The Chick-charney is said to have bent the tops of several pine trees and bound them together to form a canopy. Curt Rowlett, a merchant seaman contracted by the U.S. Navy, worked on Andros between 1984 and 1985, and reported finding one of these nests in the interior of the island.

The Chick-charney is said to have the body of a human and the face of a featherless bird, with huge round eyes, and a beak instead of a nose. The feet of a Chick-charney are three-toed claws, like those of an emu.

Local legend states that to cut down one of these nests is to invite great misfortune. According to one story, such

an incident took place at the beginning of the 20th century. Natives were reluctant to destroy a Chick-charney's nest on the plantation of a wealthy American logging merchant who had settled on the island. And rightly so, it would appear. The American insisted, so the story goes, and soon after the nest was cut down, he suffered financial ruin and met with an untimely death. The forlorn remains of what is said to be his plantation can still be seen on Andros.

### Moonlight encounter

Reported encounters with winged humanlike creatures are often very detailed; they are obviously all too real for those who experience them. One such encounter took place on a clear, moonlit summer night in 1969, near Da Nang in Vietnam. Three U.S. Marines were on guard duty on their camp perimeter. At around 1:00 A.M. the three men were sitting on top of a bunker when suddenly they saw, flying slowly toward them, a winged figure that appeared to glow with a greenish hue.

### Batwoman

One of the three Marines, Earl Morrison, who later described the incident in detail to UFO investigator Don Worley, told how, as the winged creature flew closer, he saw it was a woman with large bat wings. Morrison estimated that she must have been more than five feet tall. The batwoman was entirely black and her body seemed to be covered with what looked like fur. As the strange winged entity flew over the bunker, she made no sound. Only when she had passed about 10 feet or so beyond the Marines did they hear wings flapping.

The simplest explanation for this sighting seems to be that, given the long-term stresses of living in a war zone, the three Marines may simply have misidentified some large bird or bat. The true identity of this mysterious creature, however, remains unknown.

> **The Chick-charney is said to have the body of a human and the face of a featherless bird, with huge round eyes and a beak instead of a nose.**

# MAKALALA AND MLULARUKA

*Zoologists were astonished when, in the jungles of East Africa, a creature thought to be the stuff of legends was found living, breathing — and flying through the air.*

UNTIL THE CLOSE OF THE 19TH CENTURY, the Wasequa tribe — inhabiting a region of East Africa eight to nine days' journey from the coast of Zanzibar — claimed that their country harbored a monstrous bird. Reputedly taller than the ostrich (at eight feet the tallest bird known today), yet able to fly, it was called the *makalala* (meaning "noisy"). The bird was said to make a lot of noise when it clapped its wings, for they had hard, horny plates on their tips. The makalala was also said to be carnivorous. It was equipped with the hooked beak of a bird of prey, which it used to rip apart carrion.

## Feigning death

According to tribal lore, the Wasequas had developed a means of killing makalalas. The would-be slayer would prostrate himself upon the ground and feign death until one of these birds approached to inspect his inanimate body. He would then would leap up and kill the bird.

Science dismissed the makalala as fantasy. A bird more than eight feet tall is not easily overlooked. And if it once existed it must now be extinct, because there have been no recent reports of makalalas. The Wasequas claimed that they sometimes used makalala skulls as helmets. Evidence of the existence of this bird, in any form, however, remains to be found.

At the beginning of this century, Western visitors to what is now Tanzania in East Africa heard tales of a bizarre, unidentified creature called the *mlularuka* (meaning "flying jackal").

*Furry monster?*
*A North American flying squirrel glides through the air. A similar creature, known as the scalytail or mlularuka, has been discovered in Tanzania, in East Africa.*

According to the local inhabitants, this astonishing animal was generally seen on the wing at dusk, when it would raid the mango and pomegranate trees.

## Aerial rodent

The concept of a flying jackal was utterly discounted by zoologists until in 1926 animal collector Arthur Loveridge revealed that during an expedition to Tanzania he actually encountered a mlularuka. The so-called flying jackal proved to be a very large aerial rodent known as a scalytail (after the strange scalelike projections on its tail's underside). Between its limbs were large extensible membranes, which it used to glide through the air, so that it resembled the familiar "flying squirrels" of Eurasia and North America.

## A living legend

Scalytails had previously been documented as living in West and Central Africa, but never before in East Africa. The unveiling of Tanzania's legendary flying jackal reaffirmed that the continent of Africa's supply of zoological surprises is far from being exhausted.

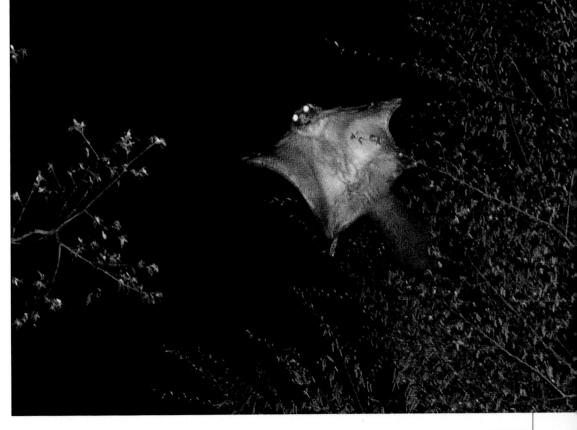

# GIANT NESTS AND EGGS

*A number of giant-sized eggs has been found, along with huge nests, all of which seems to suggest that some very large birds existed right up to recent times.*

### Living legend
*According to the Maori legends of New Zealand, monstrous birds called moas lived high in the mountains. In 1839 moa bones were found that proved these giant flightless birds actually existed. Ornithologists believe that modern kiwis, illustrated here at a moa's feet, may be closely related to this giant flightless bird.*

I N 1930 ON THE SOUTH COAST of Western Australia, where the Scott River meets the sea at Flinders Bay, 10-year-old Vic Roberts found a giant egg — 11 ½ inches long and 8 ½ inches in circumference — in sand dunes 500 yards from the sea. Vic took the egg home, where it remained until 1962, when it was seen by naturalist Harry Butler.

Butler realized that this unusual egg required scientific examination, and sent it to the Western Australian Museum in Perth. The museum's experts established that it was the egg of a bird and not a water-worn boulder or shark's egg. But the question of which native Australian bird could have produced this giant egg continued to puzzle the experts. The largest known bird in Australia is the emu, whose eggs are 13 times smaller than this find. Some experts suggested that the egg might belong to an extinct Australian bird of the Pleistocene Age, which ended about 10,000 years ago.

### Elephantine eggs
*This giant elephant bird egg was found on the island of Madagascar. The egg has a fluid capacity of about two gallons, the equivalent of the contents of 180 chicken's eggs.*

## Giant elephant bird
In 1850 some eggs of enormous size — 2 feet 8 inches long and 2 feet 2 inches in circumference — were found in a riverbed on the island of Madagascar in the Indian Ocean. Zoologists believe these eggs belonged to the giant elephant bird *Aepyornis maximus*, which is thought to have become extinct in about 1700. Fossils of the bird indicate it stood 10 feet tall and weighed just under 1,000 pounds.

Some naturalists have suggested that *Aepyornis maximus* might have laid the giant Australian egg. Harry Butler, writing in the *Science Digest* of March 1969, argued that an *Aepyornis* egg could have been carried 4,000 miles across the Indian Ocean from Madagascar and deposited

*Ostrich's egg*

*Chicken's egg*

on the Australian shore by the ocean currents. It appears unlikely, however, that an object as fragile as an egg, even a giant one, could have made such an extraordinary journey undamaged.

## Vast nests

Unaccountably large nests have also been found. In 1845 the *American Journal of Science* reported the startling discovery some years earlier, by Captain Matthew Flinders (1774–1814) of the Royal Navy, of nests on the shore of King George's Bay, off the south coast of Western Australia. These giant nests supposedly measured 26 feet in circumference, and were 32 inches in height.

In 1839 Sir Richard Owen, an eminent Victorian paleontologist, identified a giant, ostrichlike bird called the moa from bones sent to him from New Zealand. After comparing known moa bones with those found in the Australian nests, naturalists concluded that the Australian bones were those of moas. Owen believed that the moa was extinct. However, a trader named J. S. Polack, who had lived in New Zealand from 1831 to 1837, claimed he had seen bones and recent remains of moas and believed that some were still alive on the South Island of New Zealand. The Australian nests indicate that some giant birds might possibly have survived in the warmer climate of Australia.

### Height of a camel

In the early 1820's, on the other side of the world at Gebel el Zeit in Egypt, an English traveler, James Burton, discovered three colossal nests within the space of a mile. They towered to a height of 15 feet, or, as Burton observed, the height of a camel and its rider. The nests were made of a mass of heterogeneous material, including sticks, weeds, bones of fishes, and fragments of ships' timber. They seemed to be genuine, and not a man-made hoax. In one nest Burton found a human thorax and a silver watch made by the 17th-century London watchmaker George Prior. When Burton discovered them, the nests were abandoned, yet on questioning the local Arabs, Burton reportedly discovered that they had been inhabited by giant stork-like birds which had left the coast only a short time before.

The descriptions given to Burton by the local Arabs seem to match the representations of huge stork-like birds that are sculpted on the walls of the tomb of an officer in the household of the pharaoh Shufu. This pharaoh ruled over Egypt in about 2100 B.C., when such birds apparently inhabited the Nile delta. They are thought to have become extinct in about 2000 B.C.

> James Burton discovered three colossal nests. They towered to a height of 15 feet.

*Giant elephant bird's egg*

# GIANT BIRDS OF AMERICA

*With hooked beaks, razor-sharp talons, and wingspans of up to 20 feet, enormous mystery birds appear to have flown out of folklore to terrorize the inhabitants of Illinois, Missouri, Pennsylvania, and the west coast of America.*

**Carried aloft**
*Marlon Lowe, seen here with his mother, Mrs. Ruth Lowe, was allegedly carried 40 feet through the air by a large bird. Ornithologists claim that there is no known bird with claws strong enough to carry a boy four feet tall and weighing 60 pounds.*

**Its claws grasped the straps of his sleeveless shirt and lifted him off the ground. The boy shouted and hit out at his abductor with his fists.**

T 8:30 P.M. ON JULY 25, 1977, two giant birds appeared in the sky over Lawndale, Illinois. They dived and reportedly attacked three boys who were playing in the backyard of Ruth and Jake Lowe. One bird flew at 10-year-old Marlon Lowe. Its claws grasped the straps of his sleeveless shirt and lifted him off the ground. The boy shouted and hit out at his abductor with his fists. Marlon's cries brought his mother running to the scene. As she later told reporters: "I was standing at the door and all I saw was Marlon's feet dangling in the air." Mrs. Lowe screamed and the bird dropped her son after carrying him about three feet off the ground for some 40 feet. Marlon was shocked but not badly hurt.

## Graceful wings

Four adults who had rushed to the scene watched as the birds flew away. They described the creatures as coal black with white rings on their necks. They had long curved beaks and wings that were estimated to be 10 feet across. The birds were last seen flying toward some trees that lined nearby Kickapoo Creek.

Without delay Mrs. Lowe consulted books on birds at the local library to see if she could identify the bird that had tried to abduct her son. However, she could not make a positive identification. The birds' size reminded her of an ostrich, although their appearance was more like that of a condor.

## Flying south

The same birds were reported on subsequent days, flying progressively farther south in Illinois. Estimates of their wingspans ranged from 10 to 14 feet. On July 30, 1977, "Texas John" Huffer, a writer and construction worker, filmed two large birds perched in a tree by Lake Shelbyville, in southern Illinois. The film showed the birds at a distance. Ornithologists who viewed Huffer's film doubted that they were the mysterious giant birds and declared that the film showed nothing more than ordinary turkey vultures.

This declaration ended any official interest in the giant birds. Sightings continued, but people soon stopped making their reports public. Nothing as

spectacular as the Lawndale attack happened again and no other photographs were taken of these birds.

## Possible culprits

Ornithologists have continued to deny that there is any known bird of prey that could have perpetrated such an attack. The Andean condor or the California condor are the only two remotely possible candidates.

The Andean condor, the world's largest flying bird, closely fits the description of the adult witnesses at Lawndale; it has glossy black feathers with a collar of white feathers around its neck. However, the northernmost limit of its range is the southern end of the Colombian Andes, some 2,500 miles south of Illinois. The California condor is the largest flying bird in North America, but has an all-black body and pink neck, which does not tie in with the eyewitnesses' descriptions. It was also a very rare bird at the time of the attack, and since then the supposedly last wild specimen has been captured (in April 1987), making the California condor extinct in the wild.

### "The bird that devours men"

Centuries ago, only 100 miles from the site of the 1977 Illinois attack, two giant pictographs of winged creatures — called the *Piasa* (also known as "the bird that devours men") — were etched onto a cliff above the Mississippi River at Alton, Illinois. The first account of these pictographs was given by the French missionary explorer Jacques Marquette in 1673. Over time the rock flaked away and the original artwork disappeared before accurate drawings could be made. American Indians, however, would have had little difficulty in identifying the giant bird that allegedly

**Giant winged beast**
*An artist's impression of the Illinois rock painting of the fearsome* Piasa.

**Turkey vulture**
*Ornithologists believe that some sightings of mysterious big birds may simply be turkey vultures that have been misidentified.*

attempted to carry off Marlon Lowe. Indians in the Great Lakes region and in the Pacific Northwest believe in the existence of thunderbirds, powerful birds of prey with wingspans as great as 20 feet. These enormous mystery birds are so named because, according to Indian legend, the flapping of their wings was said to cause the sound of thunder.

## Mysterious disappearances

American Indian tales tell of several encounters with thunderbirds. One such bird was claimed to be responsible for the deaths of several Blackfoot Indians in Alberta, western Canada, in the mid-19th century. During a harsh winter when food was scarce, Blackfoot hunters began to vanish mysteriously. The disappearances remained a mystery until a Cree hunter named White Bear, who

> **Thunderbirds are so named because in Indian legend the flapping of their wings was said to cause the sound of thunder.**

had married into the Blackfeet, returned to tell of a harrowing experience. White Bear related how he had been carried off by a thunderbird to its nest on Devil's Head Mountain. When his abductor flew off again in search of more prey, White Bear threw himself from the nest, so the story goes, at the same time grasping hold of the legs of two thunderbird chicks he had found there. Their wings checked his fall and he reached the ground safely. He then returned to his people, who had given him up for dead.

White Bear also claimed that he had seen the bones of deer, bison, and even humans in the nest. The Blackfeet believed that the latter were all that remained of their missing hunters.

Mark A. Hall has argued in *Thunderbirds* (1988), his study of reported sightings of the big birds, that American Indian lore, pioneer encounters with big birds, and modern reports of thunderbirds, all show a consistent pattern. In North America thunderbirds are reported in the southern half of the continent in winter. In the milder months of the year they are seen in the northern half. Each spring the birds were said to return to the Great Lakes and the Pacific Northwest at the same time that thunderstorms reappeared.

## Birds of prey

Along the western edge of the continent, reports of thunderbirds show them seeming to migrate to the mountainous coastline, where they have been reported from California to Alaska. They are said to feed on small whales along the coast, while in Alaska they prey on caribou. Thunderbird nests have allegedly been discovered in the Olympic Mountains, in Washington State.

Hall also argues that the western mountains and the Appalachians in the east shelter the birds as they migrate. In the Midwest, the birds have caused great surprise and consternation by their appearances. Hall believes they are more visible there because they cannot avoid migrating over populous areas.

## History of sightings

Illinois and Missouri have a considerable history of sightings. In January 1948, in Glendale, Illinois, 12-year-old James Trares saw a bird "as big as a B-29" outside his house just before sunset. In 1977 the birds that reportedly attacked Marlon Lowe were apparently hungry

**Mythical bird**
*A wooden carving of a thunderbird made by the Haida Indians of the Pacific Northwest.*

enough to seek human prey. Hall believes they were making their annual migration south, probably returning to the region of the Ozark Mountains, Missouri, where the birds figure in rural folklore. In the spring the birds would fly north again to the area around the Great Lakes.

## Rural knowledge

In the eastern states of North America the giant birds have been seen and spoken of by country folk and rural historians. In Pennsylvania a record of the birds was compiled by local historian Robert Lyman (1894–1974). From late March into early November each year, people of north-central Pennsylvania have reported seeing the thunderbird. While many scientists persist in denying the birds' existence, and the search for bones and other remains continues, eyewitness reports suggest that something may be out there. The birds could, after all, be part of the fauna of North America.

### INCREDIBLE TERATORNS

The teratorns were remarkable Ice Age vulture-like birds that were believed to have become extinct about 10,000 years ago. Zoologists have always considered teratorns to be relatives of the New World vultures, because their bones resemble those of condors.

Bones of *Teratornis merriami*, with a wingspan of 11 to 12 feet, have been found throughout the U.S. In 1952 bones of the Incredible Teratorn (*Teratornis incredibilis*), which had a wingspan of 17 feet, were found in Nevada. Similar bones have been uncovered in California.

### Magnificent Argentine Bird

In 1980 the bones of a bird with a wingspan of 25 feet were found in central Argentina. It has been dubbed the Magnificent Argentine Bird (*Argentavis magnificens*). Its remains have been estimated to be eight million years old. This species of teratorn is the largest flying bird yet discovered.

*Biggest bird*
*Kenneth E. Campbell, one of the discoverers of the Magnificent Argentine Bird, stands in front of a silhouette of it made to scale. It is displayed in the Natural History Museum, Los Angeles.*

**Dramatic encounters**
Eyewitnesses who claim
to have seen mystery
winged creatures may
have been startled by the
unexpected appearance
of some known creature,
such as, for example,
this vampire bat.

# PREHISTORIC SURVIVORS

*Pterosaurs were prehistoric flying reptiles that lived 150 million years ago when dinosaurs walked the earth. Could modern sightings of mysterious flying reptiles be descendants of these creatures long believed to be extinct?*

*The pterosaur Rhamphorhynchus*

O N SEPTEMBER 14, 1983, at about 3:55 P.M., ambulance driver James Thompson was driving his vehicle to Harlingen, Texas, after an inspection at South Padre Island. Suddenly, his otherwise normal day ended like no other. Across the road in front of him flew the strangest creature he had ever seen. "His tail is what caught my attention," Thompson later told the *Valley Morning Star* of Harlingen. He stopped his vehicle and got out to watch it. The creature flew low over the grass. He thought the wings were five to six feet across. It had a grayish-black hide with a rough texture and no feathers. It was eight to ten feet long, including its tail. The tail was thin, ending in a "kind of fin." It had almost no neck, a hump on the back of its head, and a pouch "like a pelican's" near its throat. There was other traffic on the highway, yet no one else appeared to have seen the creature.

### Intriguing tail

For cryptozoologists the fin-like tail was the most intriguing feature of Thompson's description because it seemed to identify the animal as a *Rhamphorhynchus*, belonging to a suborder of the pterosaurs. These flying reptiles were believed to have been extinct since the late Jurassic geological period that ended about 144 million years ago. Fossils have been found that indicate that there was a species (*Rhamphorhynchus longiceps*) that grew to the size of the creature James Thompson reported.

*James Thompson*

Another dramatic sighting of a large reptilian creature from prehistoric times allegedly took place on April 20, 1890. Two cattlemen claimed that they came upon a large winged creature, with a leathery hide, in the Huachuca Desert between the Whetstone Mountains and the Huachuca Mountains outside Tombstone, in the southeastern corner of Arizona. The only contemporary record of this event was a

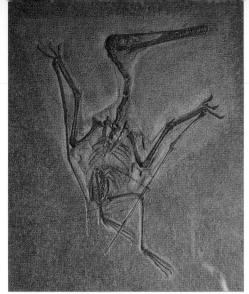

**Captured in stone**
*Preserved for approximately 150 million years in limestone, the skeleton of this pterodactyl was found at Solnhofen in Bavaria, southern Germany.*

sensational newspaper report that appeared in the Tombstone *Epitaph* on April 26, 1890. The *Epitaph* reported that the creature had allegedly a wingspan of 160 feet; the two men were said to have killed and measured the creature, and cut off its wing tip.

The report of the Tombstone monster was not investigated by zoologists at the time. There was no further evidence or follow-up stories, and the incident seemed destined to be always considered a hoax. However, when the newspaper report was resurrected in 1969, Harry F. McClure, an old man from Colorado Springs, came forward. In 1910 McClure was a young man living in Lordsburg, New Mexico, 97 miles northeast of Tombstone. McClure related a version of the story as it was told around Lordsburg when the witnesses were still living.

> ## The creature had a wingspan of 160 feet; the two men were said to have killed and measured it, and cut off its wing tip.

McClure had heard the story, had seen the two cowboys involved, and even had friends who knew them. However, after 60 years, he had forgotten the cowboys' names. McClure recalled that the two cattlemen were respected citizens and their account of events was believed by those who knew them.

### Eyes the size of saucers
According to McClure, when the two men saw the creature, it apparently came to ground some distance from them, took off, and landed again still farther away. The cattlemen estimated its wingspan as 20 to 30 feet. They claimed it had eyes the size of saucers. On the forward part of the body it had two legs and feet comparable in size to those of a

horse. The men fired at the creature with their Winchester rifles, but to no effect. While correct in some particulars, the newspaper report was clearly exaggerated and false on key points.

### A missing photograph
In the early 1960's rumors were circulating concerning a photograph published in the *Epitaph* during 1886 that depicted another mystery creature, which had supposedly been killed by two men outside Tombstone. But so many years after the event, there were different versions of what this photograph showed. Some said it showed a creature with a wingspan of 36 feet nailed to a barn wall with men dressed as cowboys standing next to it. Another version said the picture showed the creature strung up on a barbed-wire fence.

Some people who claimed to have seen the photograph likened the creature to a giant bird that resembled the thunderbird.

*The* Pteranodon

Others thought it looked more like a featherless *Pteranodon*, one of the largest types of pterodactyl, which had a wingspan of up to 25 feet. Others were just not sure how to identify what the picture showed. Moreover, anyone who remembered seeing this picture was certain of one thing: they no longer had a copy. Whether such a picture ever even existed remains uncertain.

### African flying reptiles
From the densely vegetated Jiundu Swamp in northwest Zambia, Central Africa, the world learned of another flying reptile. English explorer Frank H. Melland, in his book *In Witchbound Africa* (1923), described how he had repeatedly heard reports of a giant lizard with wings like a bat. Local travelers feared this creature, believing that to encounter it meant certain death. They called it the *Kongamato* (meaning "boat breaker")

because at certain river crossings they believed there was a danger of being attacked by it. The local Kaonde tribespeople said this creature could stop the waters flowing at fords, thus causing a sudden rise in the water level, and thereby overturning canoes.

When the locals described the Kongamato to Melland they told of a wingspan of four to seven feet, red skin, and an impressive beakful of teeth. Melland showed them pictures of pterodactyls and other animals. Without hesitation the tribespeople identified the pterodactyls as the Kongamato.

Paleontologists, who study past life on earth from fossil remains, have established that pterodactyls disappeared about 65 million years ago. When reports of sightings of such creatures persist, the question raised by cryptozoologists is: Could it be that the descendants of a small number of hardy representatives have survived into the present?

The continuing survival of giant bats in Africa became a subject of speculation in 1932. As a young man, zoologist Ivan T. Sanderson collected animals for museums. As Sanderson and a partner were shooting bats along a river in the Assumbo Mountains in Cameroon, West Africa, the young collector fell into the river while trying to hang onto a specimen. As he sought the riverbank, his partner yelled out a warning. Skimming the river's surface toward him was a large, black, winged creature about the size of an eagle. It exposed its row of teeth to Sanderson just before the naturalist ducked into the water.

### "The forked one"
The strange creature came back up the river later, but by then it had grown dark and they could only listen as the thing flew by. Sanderson thought it was a giant bat with a wingspan of 12 feet. When the collectors later described the creature to

local hunters, some shouted "*Olitiau*" before hurriedly departing. Cryptozoologist Dr. Bernard Heuvelmans has observed that Sanderson may have heard them say "*Ole ntya*" (meaning "the forked one" or "the Christian devil").

### Nocturnal animals
More has been heard about giant bats from Dutch naturalist Ernst Bartels. He grew up in western Java, Indonesia, on a tea plantation. When he was 10 years old, one of his father's assistants tried to scare him by warning him that he might be picked up and carried away to a waterfall by the dreadful *Ahool*. Later in his life, while studying a bird that nested behind waterfalls in the mountains of western Java, Bartels learned from the Sundanese people who assisted him that the *Ahool* was a genuine nocturnal animal that also spent its days in caves behind waterfalls. Its name came from the cry it made — "Ahooooool" — as it flew up and down rivers on wings 10 to 12 feet across. This was a call Bartels had heard himself. The creature was rarely seen and fed on large fish.

### Giant bats
In the 1920's and 1930's Bartels found people who had encountered the creature. He came to realize that they were describing a giant bat. It was gray, and seemed, when on the ground, to be the size of a one-year-old child. It also seemed, like most bats, to have its feet on backward. Bartels continued his research and became convinced that similar bats were to be found in Samoa, Vietnam, Madagascar, parts of East Africa, and West Africa.

### THE JERSEY DEVIL
During the week of January 16 to 23, 1909, residents of Trenton, Woodbury, Swedesboro, and many other New Jersey towns, reportedly saw a giant winged creature that flew through the night, emitting a fearsome cry. Many people also found strange hoofprints the morning after the sightings. Those who believed that they saw or heard this creature had encountered what later became known as the Jersey Devil.

### Centuries of sightings
This was not the first time that this creature apparently had been seen. American Indians reported such a devil centuries ago.

More recently, in November 1951, teenagers in Gibbstown, New Jersey, reported seeing the same creature. They heard strange noises in the woods and found maimed birds and other mammals.

Various explanations for the sightings have been put forward. One is that it is a sandhill crane, a large bird with a very strident call. Another explanation is that the creature may be a surviving *Pteranodon*, one of the largest type of pterodactyl.

**9TH AND ARCH MUSEUM**
T. F. HOPKINS ............ Manager

**CAUGHT!!! AND HERE!!! ALIVE!!!**

THE

**LEEDS DEVIL**
Captured Friday After a Terrific Struggle

EXHIBITED EXCLUSIVELY HERE AT
$1000.00 A WEEK.
The Fearful, Frightful,
Ferocious Monster Which
Has Been Terrorizing
Two States.

**Swims! Flys! Gallops!**
Exhibited Securely Chained
In a Massive Steel Cage.

**A LIVING DRAGON**
More Fearsome Than
the Fabled Monsters of Mythology.

DON'T MISS THE
SIGHT OF A LIFETIME.

BIG STRING OF
SENSATIONS IN
CURIO HALL

**THEATRE**
GRAND CONTINUOUS VAUDEVILLE

**10c ADMITS TO ALL**

*Devil on show*
*This advertisement appeared in the Philadelphia Public Ledger in 1910 to promote an entertainment based on the Jersey Devil stories.*

# FLYING SNAKES

*From the open plains of southwestern Africa, and the steamy jungles of Asia, to the bustling metropolis of central London, people have reported seeing snakes that fly.*

WHEN AN AFRIKANER FARMER's 16-year-old son did not return home from tending his father's flock near the town of Keetmanshoop in Namibia, southwestern Africa, in 1962, the farmer sent out a search party to look for him. Before long they found the youth unconscious and carried him home. When he revived, the young man was in so severe a state of shock that he was unable to speak for several days.

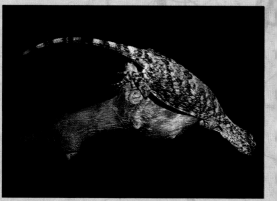

## A roaring noise

When finally he could be questioned, the youth related how he had been sitting beneath the shade of a tree carving a piece of wood when he heard a roaring noise that sounded like a mighty gust of wind. Looking up, he saw what appeared to be a giant snake hurling itself down from the mountain ridge. As the creature came closer, the noise grew deafening. The creature raised a large cloud of dust as it landed, scattering the sheep in all directions. The terrified youth remembered nothing more, because at this point he lost consciousness.

## Injured python

The sighting was investigated by South African zoologist Marjorie Courtenay-Latimer, who visited the scene of the incident a few days later. Courtenay-Latimer examined and photographed the site but could not establish any convincing explanation for what the youth had reported. She suggested that the creature he saw may have been an injured python that displayed abnormal behavior and movement.

Biochemist Dr. Roy P. Mackal, who included Courtenay-Latimer's research in his book *Searching for Hidden Animals* (1980), does not agree with the injured snake theory. This is because it does not, he says, take into account the air disturbance that accompanied the sighting. To create such atmospheric commotion, Mackal argues, some wing movement would have to be involved. Yet the boy who witnessed the flying snake never mentioned seeing any wings.

---

**Looking up, he saw what appeared to be a giant snake hurling itself down from the mountain ridge.**

---

*Essex serpent*
*In May 1669 the villagers of Henham in Essex, southeast England, allegedly saw a flying serpent. The villagers were said to have chased the snake away with sticks and stones.*

*Small flier*
*The flying lizard (Draco volans) is a small creature, usually found in Southeast Asia. It has a pair of expandable membranes on its sides that enable it to glide through the air.*

**These snakes have been seen to drop from treetop heights of up to 65 feet and land without injury. They propel themselves forward by coiling up and uncoiling suddenly, and glide through the air in an S-shape.**

Mackal argues that this creature might well have been a large, and as yet unknown, species of a small lizard that is known as the flying lizard (*Draco volans*). These animals are not uncommon in Southeast Asia. They have elongated ribs, which support expandable membranes. When the lizard's legs and tail are extended, these folds of skin stretch and so act as a kind of parachute as the animal jumps or falls.

### Gentlemanly snake

Toward the end of the 18th century there were reports of flying snakes in England, a country not otherwise noted for its variety of snakes. A reader, who signed himself S. B., described in a letter to *The Gentleman's Magazine* of April 1798 a strange snake he had seen in August 1776 a few miles west of London.

This gray mottled serpent was two feet long, the size of a common snake. "It had a pair of short wings very forward on the body, near its head....Its flight was very gentle; it seemed too heavy to fly either fast or high.... Its manner of flying was not in an horizontal attitude, but with its head considerably higher than its tail...."

### Misidentified creatures

In the same journal another correspondent, J. R., reported another winged snake that was seen on July 15, 1797, in central London. However, both these sightings may have been misidentifications of ordinary creatures, or perhaps pure hoaxes.

In another part of the world real flying snakes are known to exist. In Southeast Asia four very agile species of the tree snake *Chrysopelea* actually appear to fly. These snakes have been seen to drop from treetop heights of up to 65 feet and land without injury. They propel themselves forward by coiling up and uncoiling suddenly, and glide through the air in an S-shape. They are able to expand their ribs while compressing their bellies so that they flatten out like a ribbon, and thus they are able to glide down through the air, somewhat like a parachute.

*Flight of fancy?*
*This winged snake appeared in Edward Topsell's* Historie of Foure-footed Beastes *(1607).*

*Flying snake*
*Brightly colored tree snakes are found throughout Southeast Asia. They have been observed gliding across distances of 100 feet.*

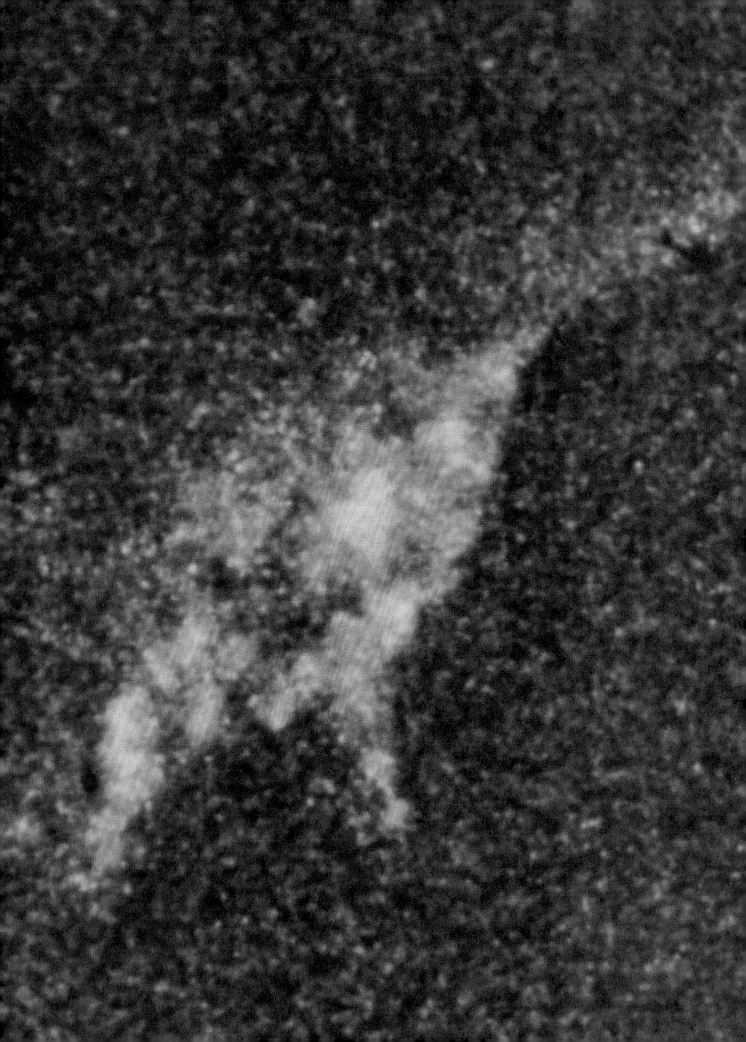

# CHAPTER TWO

# MONSTERS OF THE DEEP

*A snakelike head, a long neck, a huge body surging through the waves — this is typical of water monster sightings. Some can be attributed to imagination, others to hoaxes — yet a number of reports remain unexplained.*

In the summer of 1989 hunting guide Ernie Giroux and his wife were standing on the banks of Lake Okanagan in British Columbia. Suddenly, they reported later, they saw the upper part of a bizarre animal emerge slowly from the water. The creature had a round head "like a football," they claimed, and a neck several feet long. According to Mr. Giroux, the animal was about 15 feet long and "swam real gracefully and fast."

The Girouxs' sighting occurred at the same spot where, earlier that summer, Ken

## MONSTER THEORY

University of Chicago biochemist Dr. Roy P. Mackal has studied every reported sighting of Ogopogo, the "monster" of Lake Okanagan. From the most commonly recurring alleged features of the monster he has built up a composite picture of it. It is about 40 feet long; flexes itself vertically (producing "humps" that protrude from the water); has a tapering, sparsely bristled head, dark skin that is smooth apart from a few scaly areas, and a partly serrated back. It propels itself by up-and-down movements of a forked tail; swims rapidly, at up to 25 m.p.h.; and apparently feeds on fish.

### Primitive whales

To Mackal, all these features suggest that Ogopogo may well be a population of surviving primitive whales of the genus *Basilosaurus*. Mackal bases this idea on the characteristics of *Basilosaurus* fossils and of various living whales. He points out that whales, normally thought of as marine animals, can adapt to fresh water. For example, some dolphins (which belong to the toothed whale group) live in rivers, and in 1966 a white whale reportedly spent a month living in the River Rhine in Germany.

If Mackal's theory is correct, however, it throws into question such sightings as the Giroux's', in which Ogopogo, like the Loch Ness monster, is claimed to have a long neck.

Chaplin, a car salesman, had taken a video of what he described as a 15-foot-long, dark green, snakelike creature. Most wildlife experts who viewed the Chaplin video later reported that what it showed was probably a beaver or large river otter. But Ernie Giroux was certain that this was not what he and his wife had observed: "I've seen a lot of animals swimming in the wild, and what we saw that night was definitely not a beaver."

### Snakelike head

Lake Okanagan has reputedly been inhabited by a Loch-Ness-type monster for centuries; the Indians regarded it with superstitious dread. In 1926 the creature was first dubbed Ogopogo, a name taken from a popular English ditty.

One of the most intriguing modern sightings allegedly took place on the evening of July 17, 1959. Some friends were returning home across the lake on a motor cruiser. The man at the wheel, Mr. R. H. Miller, editor of the *Vernon Advertiser*, observed, he later claimed, an enormous animal with a snakelike head and blunt nose following the craft about 250 yards behind it. Miller turned the boat and approached to within 60 yards of the creature. The group on board later reported that they observed the animal for a full three minutes before it submerged.

### Black arch

A more recent sighting was that on the evening of August 5, 1991. Thirty staff and guests of the Lakeside Marina Hotel claimed that they saw a tremendous churning disturbance, like the wake of some object, moving up the lake, about 600 yards offshore. Carman Zieman, a jet-ski rental operator, told the press that

*Ogopogo, the Lake Okanagan monster, as depicted on a 1990 postage stamp*

the wake was about five feet high and moved against the wind at about 12 m.p.h. It was totally unlike the wake of a boat, he said. At one point, he alleged, a black object arose from the foam, "like in an arch." Others spoke of a

## The man at the wheel observed an enormous animal with a snakelike head and blunt nose following the craft.

six-foot-long hump protruding from the water. Some onlookers drove motorboats out toward the disturbance but it disappeared before they could reach it.

More than 250 lakes around the world are reputed to contain monsters. These bodies of water have several features in common. They either are connected to the sea, or were at one time; hence they

***Monster vanquished***
*Columba, a sixth-century Irish saint, seen here in the window of a church near Loch Ness, reputedly repelled an attack by the lake's monster.*

could, in theory at least, harbor migratory sea creatures. And they are usually extremely deep and cold. There are many such "monster-inhabited" lakes in the United States and Canada, one of the best known, apart from Lake Okanagan, being Lake Champlain, which is situated between New York State and Vermont. But the most famous of all such lakes is Loch Ness, Scotland, reputed home of an unidentified creature popularly dubbed Nessie.

## Nessie's sudden fame

Loch Ness, deep in the Scottish Highlands, is 24 miles long and rarely more than 1 mile wide — a modest surface area for a lake. But its enormous depth — between 750 and 1,000 feet in places — makes it the largest body of water in Britain and the third largest in Europe. Sightings of a mysterious creature in the loch have been reported for centuries (the earliest reference is in a seventh-century biography of the Irish saint, Columba), but it was not until 1933 that Nessie began to attract widespread interest. This started on May 2, when the *Inverness Courier* published a report that a local businessman and his wife had seen a strange, whale-like creature churning up water in the loch. During the following months, reports of further sightings appeared, including one by George Spicer, a company director, and his wife. They claimed that, driving past the loch on the afternoon of July 22, 1933, they saw an extraordinary, long-necked, large-bodied creature cross the road 200 yards ahead of them and disappear into the loch. They described it as "dark elephant gray, of a loathsome texture."

## Dark gray and glistening

On December 6, 1933, Nessie's growing fame became international, when newspapers around the world published the first alleged photograph of Nessie, taken the previous month by Hugh Gray, an aluminum worker. Gray said that he had watched "an object of considerable dimensions," dark gray and glistening, rise from the loch. He claimed that his photograph showed the creature when it

*First photograph*
*On November 12, 1933, Hugh Gray, a Scottish aluminum worker, took what was alleged to be the first photograph of the Loch Ness monster.*

---

**BEYOND BELIEF?**

Many alleged lake monsters conform to a fairly standard type that bears some resemblance to known animals, extinct or living. Occasionally, however, there are reports of lake monsters so bizarre that they almost defy belief. Are such creatures real, or are they merely hoaxes?

In September 1984 the Associated Press published a story about the capture in 1972 of an extraordinary animal said to have lived in Lake Duobuzhe, Tibet. Superficially, it resembled an ox, but it had short, curly horns, hippopotamus-like skin, and turtle-like legs. Allegedly, Chinese soldiers shot the creature, bayoneted it, and dragged its corpse away to a nearby village. This "hippoturtleox," as cryptozoologists (scientists who study officially unrecognized animals) have named the animal, bears no resemblance to any known creature, past or present. Since its carcass has never been found, its identity — if the report was true — is likely to remain a mystery.

**"Hippo face"**

Ten years earlier another bizarre water monster was allegedly spotted in Ireland. One day in March 1962 schoolteacher Alphonsus Mullaney and his son visited Lough Dubh, in County Galway, to fish. In the evening, according to Mr. Mullaney, he felt a sudden tugging on his line. "I hauled it slowly ashore, and the line snapped. I was examining the line when the lad screamed. Then I saw the animal. It was not a seal or anything I had ever seen. It had for instance short thick legs, and a hippo face. It was as big as a cow or an ass, square faced, with small ears and a white pointed horn on its snout. It was dark gray in colour, and covered with bristles or short hair, like a pig."

Mullaney claimed that he and his son fled. They reported what they had allegedly seen, and some local men searched for the animal. They found nothing, and since then no further sightings of such a creature have been claimed.

**Giant fish**

Far more believable than the Mullaneys' alleged monster are some giant fish claimed to have been found in Lake Hanas, Xinjiang, China. In July 1985 Prof. Xiang Lihao, a biologist at Xinjiang University, saw some enormous, reddish, salmon-like fish swimming just beneath the surface of the lake, and photographed them. Prof. Lihao has estimated that they were 30–33 feet long — more than twice the size of the previously largest known freshwater fish, a European catfish. Cryptozoologists believe that the fish may soon be granted scientific recognition.

*Nessie's flipper?*
*This underwater photograph taken on Dr. Robert Rines's expedition in 1972 allegedly shows the huge flipper of an unknown animal.*

### UNDERWATER EVIDENCE
In August 1972 a Nessie-hunting team led by Dr. Robert Rines of the Academy of Applied Science, Boston, took a striking underwater photograph with a camera suspended 45 feet below the surface. It showed what appeared to be the vast diamond-shaped flipper, measuring eight feet by four feet, of an unknown animal. Three years later, in June 1975, Rines, using sonar-activated cameras, managed to obtain an even more striking image: what could have been the long neck, small head, bulbous body, and flippers of an enormous animal.

### Name games
British naturalist Sir Peter Scott was inspired by Rines's 1972 "flipper" photograph to produce a painting of a pair of plesiosaur-like Nessies, which he exhibited in London. He later stated: "I believe that the evidence adds up to a population of large animals in Loch Ness."

Scott gave the creatures the scientific name *Nessiteras rhombopteryx*, Greek for "Ness monster with diamond fin." However, suspicions were voiced by some that Rines's photographs were a hoax. It was pointed out in the press that Scott's invented name for the creature was an anagram of "Monster hoax by Sir Peter S." Rines curtly denied this with his own anagram: "Yes, both pix are monsters. R."

was three feet out of the water, shrouded in the spray it had thrown up. Scientists were unimpressed by the picture.

Since then, many photographs alleged to be of Nessie have been published and analyzed, but, like Gray's, none has ever provided conclusive evidence that the monster exists. The clearest and most celebrated was that taken on April 1, 1934, by a London gynecologist, Dr. R. K. Wilson. Labeled "the surgeon's photograph" by the press, Dr. Wilson's picture shows, protruding from the loch, a long neck and small head resembling those of a plesiosaur, an extinct marine reptile known only from fossils.

### Joke-shop model
The Wilson photograph has been reproduced and discussed subsequently in most books on Nessie and has been regarded as one of the best proofs of the creature's existence. In 1939, for example, Roy Andrews, of the American Museum of Natural History in New York, stated categorically that it was the only known authentic photograph of the Loch Ness monster. In August 1992,

however, 58 years after the photograph was taken, a retired music teacher, Robert Wilson (no relative of Dr. Wilson), claimed that the creature in the picture was a model he had made, using a joke-shop serpent's head as its basis. Knowing when Nessie watchers would be on the lookout for the monster, he claimed, he had placed the model over his head and swum about underwater.

### Two-humped back
In all, there have been an estimated 10,000 or so reported sightings of Nessie. Some have been proven hoaxes, but investigators believe the great majority to be genuine, whether they were of a monster or not. The most commonly reported characteristics of the animals allegedly sighted are a snakelike head, a back with two humps, and a tail. A long neck and horns or antennae have also been commonly noted. The creature is often said to leave a V-shaped wash.

### Royal Air Force analysis
Many films of what is claimed to be Nessie have been shot over the years. Like the photographs, none positively establishes the existence of the animal. One of the most celebrated is the 16-millimeter-film sequence shot on April 23, 1960, by veteran Nessie-hunter Tim Dinsdale, an aeronautical engineer. Screened by BBC TV on June 13 that year, the film shows a single hump crossing the lake. Dinsdale later submitted the footage to photoanalysis

▶ PAGE 42

*Sonar sweep*
*In 1987 a flotilla of 24 boats swept Loch Ness with a sonar curtain (sound waves that reflect back from underwater objects). Known as Operation Deepscan, the sweep did not discover any firm evidence.*

# SWEDISH LEVIATHAN

***Described by one witness as slimy, scaly, and warty, a monster
has allegedly been sighted for centuries in Sweden's deepest lake.***

On August 2, 1973, fisheries officer Ragnar Björks was out in his rowboat on Sweden's Lake Storsjön, checking anglers' permits. Suddenly, he claimed, he espied a large fishlike tail protruding from the water. He rowed toward it and saw that it was part of a huge creature he estimated to be almost 20 feet long, gray-brown on top, yellow underneath.

### Boat thrown into the air
"When I was by the side of this monster," said Björks, "I took my oar and hit it straight over its back...the animal slapped the water with its tail so that the boat was thrown 3 or 4 metres [9 or 12 feet] into the air...the boat came down again on its keel but I had to balance it." Despite the shock of his encounter, Björks managed to row back to shore.

"At first I didn't believe that there was any monster in the Storsjön," said Björks, "but now I am convinced."

Lake Storsjön is Sweden's Loch Ness. Covering 176 square miles, the lake, lying in the mountains of central Sweden, is the deepest in Scandinavia, and a large unknown creature has reportedly been sighted in it since the mid-17th century. By 1898 zoologist Dr. Peter Olsson had collected 22 accounts of 19th-century sightings of the creature. The first dated from 1820, when a farmer claimed that a strange animal had followed his boat. A housepainter who saw it in the 1830's called it the Storsjön Leviathan.

### Water disturbance
From the collected reports emerged a composite picture of the creature: shaped like an upturned boat, hump-backed, fast-moving, and causing tremendous water disturbance. In four reports the monster was described as having a smooth, round, doglike head, with large eyes.

> "I took my oar and hit it straight over its back...the animal slapped the water with its tail so that the boat was thrown 9 or 12 feet into the air."

One of the most detailed and fascinating accounts of the Storsjön monster was given by newspaper researcher P. E. Asen, who claimed to have seen it on July 10, 1898, with five other people. At first, he said, he thought it was a capsized boat, but, upon rowing out to it, he saw that it was a very large animal, whose head and neck were submerged. Head and neck, Asen alleged, were together 5 feet long and the body was 13–16 feet long and 4 feet high. According to Asen, the creature's head had two white "ears" or "fins" (noted by other observers), and the body was cinnamon-brown, slimy, scaly, and warty, with protuberances along its spine, from which hung green waterweed or perhaps a mane. After he had watched it for about an hour, Asen claimed, the creature was disturbed by a lake steamer's whistle and disappeared.

### Stranded sea monster?
Since 1987 a Swedish organization, the Society for Investigating the Great Lake, has accumulated about 400 reports of sightings of the Storsjön monster. As with the Loch Ness monster, one theory advanced to account for the creature's supposed presence in the lake is that it may be a marine species that migrated there and was then cut off from the sea approximately 10,000–20,000 years ago, during the last Ice Age.

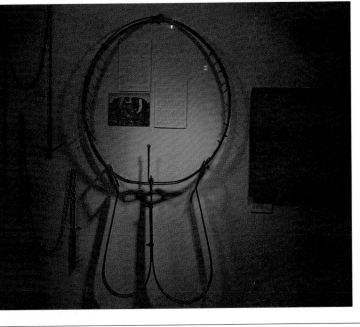

***Untried trap***
*These harpoons and large spring-jawed trap, exhibited in the museum of Ostersund, Sweden, were made in the 1890's to catch the monster. They were never put to use.*

experts at the Royal Air Force's Joint Aerial Reconnaissance Intelligence Centre. They concluded that the hump was 12–16 feet wide and 5 feet high (indicating that if it belonged to a predominantly submerged creature, this would be huge), that it could not have been a boat, and that it was "probably...an animate object."

### Probing the depths

Dedicated Nessie-hunters over the years have included Robert Love, who in 1969 made early sonar probes of the loch; Dr. Robert Rines, of the Academy of Applied Science, Boston, who in 1975 carried out extensive sonar-activated underwater photography; Adrian Shine, who in 1987 supervised the high-tech Operation Deepscan, a flotilla of 24 boats that made a sonar sweep of the loch; and Project Urquhart, a three-year joint venture launched in 1992 to make a scientific survey of the loch.

Various theories have been advanced as to what Nessie might be. It has been suggested that the monster is a primitive whale, a long-necked seal, a giant eel or worm, a walrus, a floating mass of vegetation, a diving bird, or a family of otters. But the most popular theory is that Nessie is a plesiosaur. This marine reptile, which had a small head, long neck, and large flippers, has supposedly been extinct for 60–70 million years. Some scientists, however, believe that the loch may once have been connected to the sea. It may, they theorize, have become cut off during the last Ice Age, 10,000–20,000 years ago, with the result that migratory plesiosaurs may have been stranded in it.

On the other hand, some researchers, such as zoologist Dr. Maurice Burton and Ronald Binns, author of *The Loch Ness Mystery Solved*, have suggested that all the evidence advanced for Nessie's existence is much too vague or flawed to have any true scientific value, and have

> ## The most popular theory is that Nessie is a plesiosaur, a marine reptile supposedly extinct for 60–70 million years.

### Hunting the monster
*Lake Champlain Phenomena Investigation is engaged in a long-term, and intensive, search for the lake's supposed monster, known as Champ. Here a member of the group prepares his scuba gear, ready to continue the search.*

### Champ in the viewfinder?
*One of the most famous of alleged lake monster photographs is this one of Champ, the Lake Champlain monster, taken in 1977 by Sandra Mansi.*

concluded that the animal probably does not exist. Yet their opinions have failed to dissuade those researchers who argue that the thousands of Nessie sightings over the centuries cannot simply be dismissed, and that some creature does inhabit the murky depths of the loch.

### American Nessie

Lake Champlain, a 109-mile-long waterway, has been called America's Loch Ness. There have been about 250 sightings of its alleged monster (nicknamed Champ), many being of a strange creature with a long, sinuous neck and dark, humped body, 15–25 feet long. The best-known photograph alleged to be of Champ is that taken on July 5, 1977, by Sandra Mansi of Connecticut and published four years later in *The New York Times*. It shows a creature's small head and long neck emerging from the lake, remarkably like those in the supposed photograph of Nessie taken in 1934 by Dr. Wilson.

Theories about the identity of Champ are much like those advanced to explain Nessie. Joseph Zarzynski, a social studies teacher, who founded Lake Champlain Phenomena Investigation, believes that the plesiosaur is the most likely candidate. He and Jim Kennard of Rochester Engineering Laboratories have used high-tech sonar to search for Champ, and on June 3, 1979, one reading indicated the presence of a 10–15-foot-long moving object in the lake.

# THE PATAGONIAN LAKE MONSTER

## *"Then the water-skiers...started skiing this side of the monster. And the monster still looked magnificent, and high above them by a long way. Well that really shook us: I began to tremble."*

A MONSTER CALLED NAHUELITO is reputed to dwell in Nahuel Huapi, a lake in Patagonia, Argentina. When Tom Vernon, a British traveler, writer, and filmmaker, was cycling through Patagonia in 1989, making a television program, he met a woman who claimed to have seen the monster in all its awesome grandeur. What follows is his account of his interview with her, taken from his book *Fat Man in Argentina* (1990).

"Nahuelito...is said only to appear in a flat calm.... I went to see Mrs. Hilda Rumboll, who had [seen it], 14 years before...her family was noted for its interest in natural history: and her eldest son was a well-known professional in the field....From the window in her house I could see across the lake. It was 17 kilometres wide there, she said, and 450 metres deep.

### Enormous wash

"'It was a day with no wind [said Mrs. Rumboll]. Over there, at the beginning of the lake, more or less, an enormous wash took place. I've never seen anything like it — it must have been the height of this wall. The monster came in with a terrific rush, and settled. The huge wake was slowing down, and the water was calming — and suddenly there he was, swimming in the water with his head in the air. So I marked him by that tree, rushed straight off and got my husband, and we sat from 12 to 15 minutes watching the animal....

"'Then the water-skiers came out after lunch and started skiing this side of the monster. And the monster still looked magnificent, and high above them by a long way. Well, that really shook us: I began to tremble....

### Hefty tail

"'The head wasn't big in comparison, but the length of neck was frightening. But then, my word! The creature suddenly decided, "I've had enough of sunshine, I'll go down below again." So it switched all the way round. Every bit of water was in motion — all round as far as you could see. It disturbed the whole lake. And how can a tail rock the whole of a lake unless it's something pretty hefty?...'

"'So it was a very active sort of monster?' I suggested.

"'Oh, terribly fast — I've never seen anything quicker. But it went down slowly just like the periscope of a submarine, and I didn't see another thing.'"

# A LIVING DINOSAUR?

*From the depths of central Africa reports have emerged that a giant reptilian creature inhabits the area's unexplored swampland. Some scientists believe that it may be a surviving dinosaur.*

I N A HISTORY of central Africa, published in 1776, Abbé Proyart, a French priest, reported that a strange beast was rumored to live in the swampland of the region: "Missionaries, while passing through a forest, observed the track of an animal which they did not see but which must have been monstrous: the marks of the claws were noted on the ground, and these formed a print about three feet in circumference. The arrangement of the impressions indicated that the animal was walking not running; the distance between the footprints measured seven to eight feet." This description suggests a creature midway in size between a rhinoceros or hippopotamus and a small forest elephant — but none of these has claws.

## Undisturbed by time

Since then there have been many sightings of the missionaries' "monstrous animal," which the Africans call Mokele-mbembe. Cryptozoologists have asked the question: Could Mokele-mbembe be a living dinosaur?

The unexplored swamps of central Africa have changed very little since the end of the Cretaceous geological period, some 65 million years ago, which is when, according to the fossil record, dinosaurs were believed to have disappeared from the earth. Over that vast stretch of time the area has been scarcely disturbed by geological forces or by man. If one or more dinosaurs had managed to survive the general extinction, their most likely habitat, it is suggested, would be a region such as this untouched swampland.

Over the years various explorer-scientists, fired by the hope of catching a surviving dinosaur, have searched the area for evidence of Mokele-mbembe. In 1980 Dr. Roy P. Mackal, a biochemist, engineer, and biologist, of the University

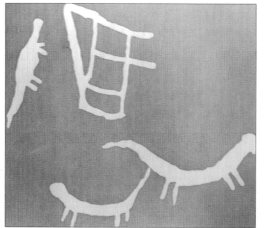

***Swampland sightings***
*From earliest times tales of dragons have emerged from the swamplands of the Congo Republic. Modern sightings of a mystery animal, indicated on this map by red dots, suggest that, if it does exist, it resembles the thin-necked dinosaur Apatosaurus.*

***Primitive image***
*African rock paintings from a cave near Mpika, Zambia, depict animals unlike any known living creatures. The one at the top left of this picture resembles certain long-necked dinosaurs.*

of Chicago, and James Powell, a crocodile expert, mounted an expedition to the previously unexplored Likouala swamps of the Congo Republic, from which had emerged reports of various strange animals.

On their travels through the unexplored swampland, Mackal and Powell gathered from natives many eyewitness accounts of sightings of Mokele-mbembe. The animals allegedly seen have the appearance of a giant reptile. They have a body the size of a small elephant; a snakelike head and long, flexible neck (sometimes with a frill along the back of both); a long, muscular, crocodilian tail; and short legs (the hind ones three-clawed). Their overall length is 15–30 feet, and their color is most commonly described as brownish-red. They are said

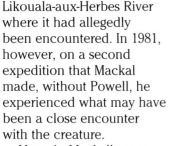

the scenery, or perhaps even in the atmosphere....
There was a pervasive sense of traveling back to the
time when the world was young, a hothouse or
maybe a Garden of Eden....

### Great "plop"

"As the expedition dugouts rounded a bend in the
river, coming close to the right-hand shore where great
jungle trees rose 120 feet above the river, everywhere
one saw Malombo, the supposed food of the Mokele-
mbembe. To the left, the jungle canopy was abruptly
broken by a bright sunlit expanse of elephant grass,
comprising a small savanna, where the bank rose a
surprising five feet above the river surface. The water
inshore was in the shadow of the elevated bank. Then
a great 'plop' sound was heard. A wave cresting at
10 inches washed over the dugout, directly from the
bank of the shadowed area. The pygmies screamed
hysterically: 'Mokele-mbembe, Mokele-mbembe!'

### Submerged creature

"Pastor Thomas, the expedition interpreter, swung the
dugout around in an arc toward shore, almost shipping
water. The great creature, which had suddenly
submerged, was nowhere in sight. Subsequent probing
revealed a shallow shelf just beneath the river surface,
which dropped off sharply to a depth of 25 feet. The
animal was probably standing on the shallow shelf
when the sudden appearance of the dugout and the
noise of the outboard motor startled it....

"No one, except the pygmies, claimed to have had
more than a fleeting impression of the great creature.
However, everyone agreed that it could not have been
a hippopotamus, elephant, or crocodile."

After several years of investigation Mackal came to
the conclusion that: "Whenever eyewitness observers
of the Mokele-mbembe were presented with illustrations
of known living and extinct animals, they unhesitatingly
selected pictures of sauropod [long-necked] dinosaurs
as representing the Mokele-mbembe. The fact that all
first-hand descriptions...are remarkably consistent
suggests that what are
being described are
real animals."

to utter no sounds and to leave round footprints about
12 inches across. The creatures reportedly feed on the
fruit of the climbing Malombo vine *Landolphia mannii*,
which is known to have grown in Cretaceous times.

Mackal and Powell never saw Mokele-mbembe
themselves but were shown various sites along the
Likouala-aux-Herbes River
where it had allegedly
been encountered. In 1981,
however, on a second
expedition that Mackal
made, without Powell, he
experienced what may have
been a close encounter
with the creature.

Here, in Mackal's own
words, is what happened:
"As we moved downstream on
the Likouala-aux-Herbes River,
everyone gradually became
aware of a subtle change in

***In search of a dinosaur***
*In 1981 Dr. Roy P. Mackal
(center, holding rifle) made his
second expedition to the Likouala
swamplands to search for the
alleged living dinosaur Mokele-
mbembe.*

# TERRORS BENEATH THE WAVES

*Tales of horrifyingly large sea serpents and other monstrous creatures lurking in the ocean depths have always held a morbid fascination for man. But is there any basis for them in reality?*

O N JULY 30, 1915, off the coast of France, the German submarine *U-28* torpedoed the British steamer *Iberian*. The vessel rapidly sank. Shortly afterward there was a tremendous explosion, and water shot 100 feet into the air. According to the U-boat commander, Georg Freiherr von Forstner, the fountain of water was seen to contain not only fragments of the *Iberian* but also an enormous sea serpent, some 60 feet long and somewhat resembling a crocodile. Falling back into the sea, the awesome creature writhed on the surface for a while, claimed Forstner, then sank completely out of sight.

### Worldwide reports
Forstner's was only one of many alleged sightings of sea serpents that have been reported down the centuries. Before the 18th century most such stories emanated from Scandinavia. (In his *Natural History of Norway* [1752–53] Erik Pontoppidan, bishop of Bergen, declared that, as the result of his inquiry into hundreds of these claimed sightings, he was reluctantly forced to believe in the existence of sea serpents.) However, in the 18th century there were numerous reports of these creatures from various parts of the globe, including the United States, where several alleged sightings were made off the coast of Maine.

### The "Stronsay monster"
Occasionally, the stranded corpse of an enormous marine animal has provoked debate about the reality of sea serpents. In 1808, on the small Orkney island of Stronsay, off the coast of Scotland, fisherman John Peace noticed on some rocks what he took to be a dead whale. Closer inspection showed that the creature had a small head, long neck, thin tail, and paired fins or feet. Some days later the rotting carcass was washed up on to the beach. It measured 55 feet from nose to tail, and the neck was 15 feet long.

An official inquiry attempted to establish the true identity of the Stronsay monster, as it came to be known, but, before accurate scientific drawings could be made, most of the carcass was swept away in a storm. However, the skull, some vertebrae, and a few other fragments were salvaged, and marine

> **Falling back into the sea, the creature writhed on the surface for a while...then sank completely out of sight.**

*Fearsome predator*
*The deep-sea fish* Pseudoscopelus *can devour prey twice its own size. It is possible that much larger, even more awesome creatures live in the unexplored ocean depths.*

## MEGAMOUTH

On November 15, 1976, off Hawaii, the U.S. research vessel *AFB-14* hauled its two great parachute anchors to the surface from a depth of 540 feet. Entangled in one was a giant shark, 14 1/2 feet long and weighing 1,653 pounds. It had protruding jaws and a great gaping mouth containing more than 200 rows of small teeth. The strange creature was brought aboard and taken to the Naval Undersea Center, Hawaii. There marine biologists pronounced it to be a unique shark, for which they had to invent not only a new genus and species but even a new family.

The scientists named the creature *Megachasma pelagios*, meaning "yawning mouth of the open sea" – but it was soon popularly dubbed Megamouth. Its huge maw enabled it to filter large amounts of plankton from the sea.

### Vertical migrator

Since then, several other specimens of Megamouth have been caught, some even larger. Scientists were initially astounded that such a creature should have remained undetected until the late 20th century. But, upon observing the movements of a specimen fitted with sonic transmitters, they discovered that Megamouth was a vertical migrator, moving to near the surface only at dusk and plunging to great depths at dawn. This probably explained why there were no previous sightings of the animal. It also lent further weight to the possibility that deep in the ocean there are many more giant creatures as yet unknown to man.

***Fake remains***
*"Sea monster" remains sold in the United States in the 19th century were usually nothing more than dismembered whales.*

biologists concluded that they were the remains of a large basking shark.

When the tissues of such a shark decompose, the extensive gill area quickly rots away, taking the jaws with it and leaving little more in front of the pectoral fins than the cranium and spinal column. Dried fibers from the surface muscles resemble a fringe of hairs, and the cartilage of the two reproductive claspers, together with the pectoral and pelvic fins, give the impression of three pairs of legs. The overall result is that the corpse resembles some serpentine sea monster.

The lessons drawn from the remains of the "Stronsay monster" were soon forgotten, however, and over the years similar carcasses gave rise to further reports of sea serpents having been stranded ashore: among others, in New Jersey, in 1822; in British Columbia and near Cherbourg, France, in 1934; and in the Orkneys again, in 1941. But however

much a dead basking shark may resemble a dead sea serpent, it cannot account for the many alleged sightings of live sea serpents reported from all around the world. Most alleged sea serpents are seen by only a few people, but in August 1817 one was apparently seen in the harbor of Gloucester, Massachusetts, by so many eyewitnesses that its reality seemed beyond doubt. All the observers described the animal as about 60 feet long, dark brown, snakelike, many-humped, and capable of moving at about 45 m.p.h. Some claimed to have approached it so closely by boat that they could touch it with their oars. Reportedly, it came ashore, was hit by musket fire but was unharmed, and stayed in the area for three weeks.

### Many eyewitnesses

Following the Gloucester sightings, hoaxes were perpetrated for many years. However, during the 19th century there were also, apparently genuine reports of sea-serpent sightings. None was taken more seriously or became more celebrated than that recorded by Peter M'Quhae, captain of the British corvette

***Mass sighting***
*In 1817 many eyewitnesses reported seeing a sea serpent in Gloucester harbor, Massachusetts. The monstrous creature is shown here in a contemporary engraving.*

***Motley monsters***
*This old map of Iceland is illustrated with an assortment of weird imagined sea monsters, each made up of parts of known animals.*

H.M.S. *Daedalus*. It was 5:00 P.M. on August 6, 1848, and the ship was southeast of the island of St. Helena in the Atlantic when the captain and some officers and crew allegedly saw, approaching the ship, "an enormous serpent, with head and shoulders kept about four feet constantly above the surface of the sea." The observers claimed that it passed within 200 yards of the ship, moving rapidly on a straight

---

## Captain and crew allegedly saw "an enormous serpent" 60 feet long.

---

course and against a cross sea. M'Quhae estimated the visible body to be at least 60 feet long. It was dark brown, with a yellowish-white throat, he said, had a clearly observable eye, nostril, and mouth, was level-backed, and did not undulate as it moved.

Some scientists, attempting to interpret the *Daedalus* sighting, proposed that the alleged serpent was in fact a giant squid or blue whale. Sir Richard Owen, the eminent British paleontologist, claimed in *The Times* that the creature must have been a seal — but M'Quhae protested that he knew the difference between a seal and a serpent. The result of M'Quhae's testimony was that claimed sea-serpent

sightings were no longer ridiculed in Britain, and over the next 40 years two-thirds of all such sightings were British.

### Monthly sightings

From the second decade of this century sea serpents have often allegedly been seen off the west coast of North America, particularly around Vancouver Island, where there were almost monthly sightings from the 1930's to the 1960's. A survey of observations of large unidentified marine animals conducted in British Columbia in 1969–70 concluded that 23 recent sightings could not be accounted for by any known animals. Since March 1987, however, there have been no sightings, and those who believe in the existence of a local sea serpent fear that it may have become extinct.

### THE CLEARWATER MONSTER

In February 1948 a resident of Clearwater, Florida, on the Gulf of Mexico, drew attention to some giant footprints on the beach. Each was 14 inches long and 11 inches wide, with three claw marks. Whatever had made these tracks had apparently emerged from the Gulf and, taking 4-foot to 6-foot strides, had walked along the beach for about two miles before returning to the sea.

Further tracks were then found on other beaches and on river banks. After a two-week study of some of them, zoologist Ivan T. Sanderson concluded, in a 50-page report, that they had probably been made by a giant penguin, about 15 feet tall. A hoax, he said, was out of the question: Any specially made artificial feet would have weighed a ton each, far too heavy to be used to make such huge strides.

### Mystery solved

For 40 years the mystery remained. Then, on June 11, 1988, in the *St. Petersburg Times*, writer Jan Kirby revealed the solution. A Clearwater resident, Tony Signorini, admitted to her that the footprints were a hoax that he had perpetrated with a friend, Al Williams, who was now dead. Signorini showed Kirby two large, three-toed, cast-iron feet, each weighing 30 pounds, which he and Williams had worn to make the prints. To make the long strides, said Signorini, "I would just swing my leg back and forth, then give a big hop, and the weight of the feet would carry me that far."

*Tony Signorini wearing the cast-iron "monster" feet*

# GIANT SERPENTS
# OF THE SEA

*The oceans of the world have never been fully explored, and it may be that lurking within their depths are giant serpents and other creatures as yet unknown to man. We present here some images of these monsters produced, over the years, from eyewitness accounts.*

**Head lines**
In 1848 a celebrated sighting of a supposed sea serpent was made from the British ship *Daedalus*. This drawing of its head was based on sketches made by Peter M'Quhae, captain of the vessel.

**Destructive force**
A sea serpent was reported in 1819 to have destroyed a ship off the coast of Boston, Massachusetts. Distorted re-tellings of the story and the artist's lively imagination combined to produce this nightmarish lithograph of the event.

**Galveston giant**
In 1872 a great sea serpent — shown here in an illustration from *The World of Wonders* (1875) — was reportedly sighted off Galveston, Texas.

THE SEA-SERPENT, AS SEEN OFF GALVESTON IN 1872.

### Mariners' fears

The seafarers of Venice, a great maritime city, had the mariner's typical fears of unknown sea creatures. This Venetian map of 1539 depicts a sea serpent destroying a ship.

### Traveler's tale

The sea serpent Physeter attacks the vessel and crew of Auriol, one of the four Brother Knights of Sicily. This illustration is from an interpretation of the medieval traveler's tale in *The World Wonderful* (1898) by the English writer Charles Squire.

### Norwegian nightmare

Two churchgoers of Heroy, Norway, are pursued across a fjord by a terrifying sea serpent. The illustration is from *Natural History of Norway* (1752–53) by Erik Pontoppidan, bishop of Bergen.

### Naturalists' blunder

In 1817 the Linnaean Society of New England declared this hump-backed snake to be a sea serpent, which they called *Scoliophis atlanticus*. It was in fact a deformed blacksnake.

# TENTACLES OF DEATH

*Giant squids, enormous jellyfish — such deadly and terrifying creatures were once thought to be simply the products of fevered imaginations. But over the years proof has emerged that they do exist.*

*I*N 1874, IN THE BAY OF BENGAL, a crewman aboard the steamer *Strathowen* was scanning the sea through binoculars when he saw a giant squid ram the becalmed 150-ton schooner *Pearl* and seize it in its tentacles. Three of the crew slashed at it with axes, but the squid's weight apparently shifted the ballast, making the ship heel over and sink, leaving few survivors.

## Pulpy mass
Just as terrifying an incident occurred in January 1973, when the 1,483-ton vessel *Kuranda* ran into heavy seas north of Australia. The ship's cargo shifted in the hold and the entire bow began dipping beneath the waves. Suddenly, after one particularly steep pitch, the vessel caught with its bow a truly enormous lion's mane jellyfish. Estimated to weigh about 20 tons, the gigantic

> **American whalers told of finding in the stomachs of slaughtered sperm whales squids' arms as thick as ships' masts.**

jellyfish covered the deck two feet deep with its pulpy mass. Its great poisonous tentacles swirled across the vessel's superstructure, enveloping the wheelhouse. One tentacle caught a seaman named McGiniss, who screamed in agony and died minutes later. The captain and the rest of the crew sheltered below decks....

Eventually, the deep-sea salvage tug *Hercules* arrived in response to a radio distress call from the *Kuranda*. It took the *Hercules* two hours, using high-pressure steam hoses, to wash most of the jellyfish loose.

## Enormous arms
One of the fanciful monsters of Scandinavian folklore was the terrible kraken, which had a body a mile and a half in circumference and enormous arms capable of dragging the largest ship to the bottom of the sea. Though grossly exaggerated, the tales were evidently based on seamen's encounters with giant squids. American whalers, too, told of finding in the stomachs of slaughtered sperm whales squids' arms as thick as ships' masts. Yet naturalists consigned all such stories to the realm of fantasy — until the 19th century, when

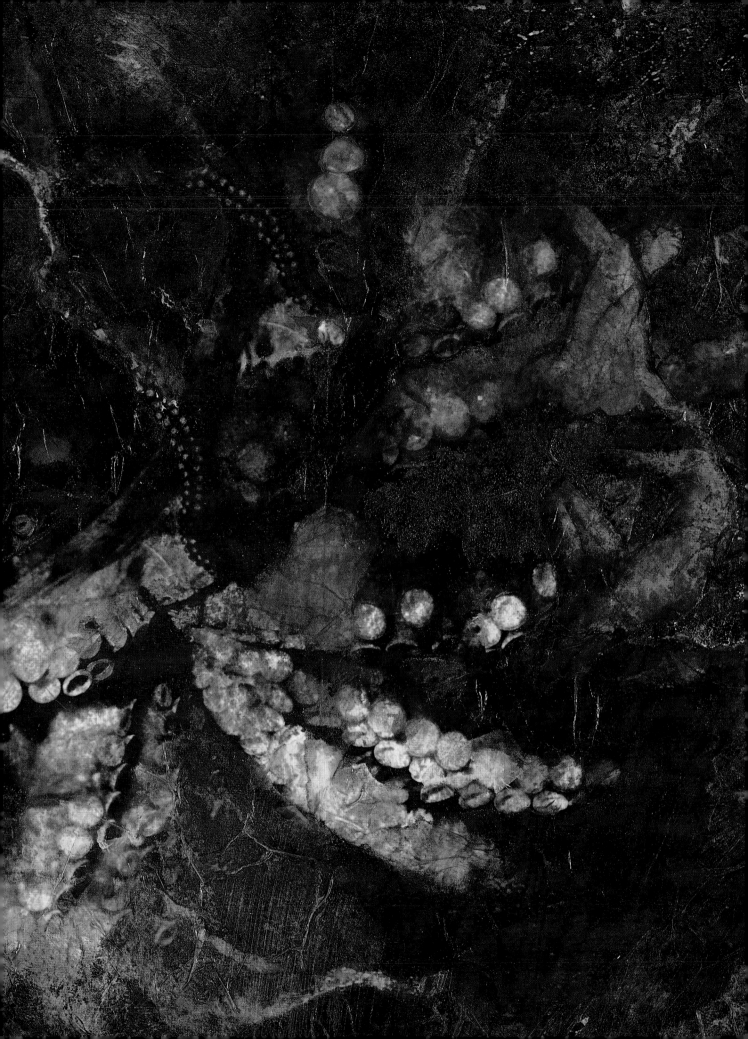

**Fishermen attacked**
*A giant octopus attacks a fishing boat from Jersey, an island in the English Channel. The illustration is from a 1922 edition of the Italian magazine* Illustrazione del Popolo.

physical evidence of the existence of giant squids began to mount. In December 1853 a large sea animal was washed ashore in Denmark. Its body was used for bait before it could be scientifically examined, but its large throat and horny beak were rescued. Prof. Johan Japetus Steenstrup, a zoologist at Copenhagen University, identified the remains as part of a giant squid, firm evidence for him that the kraken had a zoological origin.

Eight years later a giant squid was almost captured. On November 30, 1861, off the Canary Islands, the French warship *Alecton* encountered a huge, brick-red, floating squid with eyes the size of plates. The commander, Frédéric-Marie Bouyer, estimated the creature's head and body to be about 20 feet long and its arms another 5 feet long. Its tentacles (two separate prey-catching structures) were missing. It emitted a strong smell, and the general opinion was that it might be dying. After unsuccessful attempts to shoot and harpoon it, the crew slipped a noose around it, but this simply snapped off the end of the tail, and the creature escaped. The portion of tail was taken to Tenerife, from where a full report was sent to the Academy of Sciences in Paris.

### Chopped off arm
In October 1873 three fishermen in Conception Bay, Newfoundland, stuck a boat hook into a massive floating squid, which immediately attacked them. Twelve-year-old Tom Piccot chopped off one of the animal's arms and one of its tentacles with an ax, and, in a cloud of ink, the squid sank out of sight. The fishermen reckoned that the animal's body was 12 feet long and its overall length 44 feet. Piccot kept his piece of tentacle, which was 19 feet long and 3 $\frac{1}{2}$ inches in circumference, but later sold it to Moses Harvey, a local naturalist. Weeks later, Harvey acquired a giant

squid that had been caught in a herring net and decapitated. Photographs were published of it draped over a bathtub.

### Monstrous sizes
Over the years giant squid have been regularly sighted off Newfoundland, New Zealand, Japan, and elsewhere, and a few have been found stranded. The largest scientifically recorded squid is one washed up in November 1878 in Thimble Tickle Bay, Newfoundland. This creature had a body length of 20 feet and an overall length of 55 feet. Nine years later a squid 57 feet long ran aground in Big Bay, New Zealand, but its great length was accounted for mainly by its tentacles: its body was only 8 feet long. These are vast sizes, but marine biologists believe that the world's oceans may hold specimens even more monstrous.

### Massachusetts jellyfish
The largest scientifically observed jellyfish is a specimen of *Cyanea arctica*, examined in Massachusetts in 1865, which had 120-foot-long tentacles. The lion's mane jellyfish draped over the *Kuranda*, however, was estimated by the second officer of the ship to have tentacles 200 feet long. It may be that even larger specimens also exist. In

---

## Three fishermen stuck a boat hook into a massive floating squid, which immediately attacked them. It was 44 feet long.

---

November 1969 two skin divers, Richard Winer and Pat Boatwright, were 30–40 feet deep in the ocean off Bermuda when they saw an enormous, round, pulsating, pink-edged, purple creature beneath them. Winer thought that it was a monstrous jellyfish. The two men estimated its body to be somewhere between 50 and 100 feet across. Since the Massachusetts jellyfish had a body only 7 $\frac{1}{2}$ feet across, the Bermuda specimen's tentacles would presumably have been of extraordinary proportions.

# BLOBS AND GLOBSTERS

*On beaches in Florida, Bermuda, and Australasia great masses of unidentified animal tissue have been washed up. Are they the remains of giant sea creatures as yet unknown to science?*

ON NOVEMBER 30, 1896, TWO YOUNGSTERS cycling on Anastasia Beach, near St. Augustine, Florida, came across an enormous, pale, silvery pink mass of what appeared to be decomposing animal tissue. They immediately reported their find to a local physician and natural historian, Dr. DeWitt Webb, who, with others, examined the carcass. They discovered that it was about 23 feet long, 18 feet across, and 4 feet high, and weighed about five tons. Along its sides were what appeared to be the stumps of five or six great arms — one investigator claimed to have found fragments of arms up to 32 feet long in the surrounding sand.

### Tremendous tentacles
The carcass, and alleged arms, were washed out to sea by a storm. Although the former was cast back on shore two miles south, the arms were never seen again. Prof. A. E. Verrill, a zoologist of Yale University, eventually decided the remains were those of a giant octopus previously unknown to science. He estimated that, when alive, its tentacles would have been 75–100 feet long, an enormous size: The tentacles of the largest scientifically measured octopus were 11 1/2 feet long.

But upon examination of tissue samples taken from the creature Prof. Verrill changed his mind, concluding that they probably came from the head of a sperm whale. However, many years later, in 1963, Dr. Joseph Gennaro, of the University of Florida, reexamined the samples under the microscope and decided that the tough, pale, fibrous tissue was unlike the tissue of a whale or squid but did resemble that of an octopus. In the early 1980's biochemist Dr. Roy P. Mackal analyzed the amino acids (the chief components of proteins) in the samples and also concluded that these probably came from a giant octopus of an unknown species.

> They discovered that the creature was about 23 feet long, 18 feet across, and 4 feet high, and weighed about five tons. Along its sides were what appeared to be the stumps of five or six great arms.

### Bermuda Blob
Since then another large, mysterious organic mass has been washed ashore. In May 1988, fisherman Teddy Tucker discovered the remains of a creature on his beach in Mangrove Bay, Bermuda. The object was about eight feet long and "very rubbery." Tucker took color photographs of it and, before it was washed out to sea, cut off a sample and sent it to Dr. Eugenie Clark, a marine biologist at the University of Maryland.

Analysis of the sample indicated that it consisted of collagen (a tough, fibrous protein that is the main component of connective tissue) and that it originated from a large, cold-blooded vertebrate such as a fish or reptile. Some zoologists have suggested that the Bermuda Blob, as it is popularly called, may be similar to the Florida carcass and may also be the remains of a giant octopus. But this is only speculation, and the Blob's identity remains a mystery.

It is also not known if there is any connection between the Florida and Bermuda carcasses and three mysterious organic masses that in the 1960's were washed ashore on beaches in Tasmania and New Zealand. Dubbed globsters by zoologist Ivan T. Sanderson, these ranged in length from 8 to 30 feet and were all described as tough, rubbery, and odorless, with a hairy or "stringy" outer covering. Naturalists were unable to relate them to any known animals.

*The Bermuda Blob*
*Teddy Tucker probes the Bermuda Blob he found in shallow water in Mangrove Bay, Bermuda. According to Tucker, cutting into the Blob was "like trying to cut a car tire."*

# CHAPTER THREE

# MORE BEAST THAN MAN

*Humans are fascinated by the animals, such as gorillas and chimpanzees, that seem closest to them in behavior and intelligence. Intriguing reports of similar apelike creatures, thus far unknown to science, continue to emerge from the world's wildernesses.*

At about 3:30 P.M. on Friday, October 20, 1967, Roger Patterson and Bob Gimlin were riding on horseback through the wilderness area of Bluff Creek, northeast of Eureka, California. Suddenly, they claimed, they came upon "a sort of man-creature" crouched over a fallen tree trunk beside the creek about 100 yards away from them.

Patterson's horse took fright and reared up, unseating its rider. Startled by this commotion, the bizarre figure turned

## BIGFOOT IN THE FRAME

In 1971 Roger Patterson's alleged film of a Bigfoot was analyzed by specialists in human locomotion. After examining the film, Donald Grieve, reader in biomechanics at the Royal Free Hospital of Medicine, London, concluded that the movie's authenticity depended on the speed at which it had been filmed. If the movie had been shot at 24 frames per second (fps) then the subject could be a large, walking man. If it had been shot at 18 fps, a human being would be unable to match the movements observed in the film.

Patterson claimed that, on checking his camera, he found that it was at a setting of 18 fps.

### Jumpy film

Soviet scientists at the Central Institute of Physical Culture in Moscow worked out an ingenious method of calculating the speed at which Patterson's film had been shot — and the result seemed to confirm Patterson's claim. The jumpy nature of the film recorded the rate of Patterson's stride as he ran toward the creature.

The scientists calculated that, if the film had been shot at 24 fps, then Patterson would have been taking six strides per second — a pace faster than that of a world-class sprinter. They therefore concluded that the film must have been shot at 18 fps.

and stood up. Large, hairy, and heavyset, the creature appeared to be of a considerable size and was also immediately recognizable as female, for its breasts were large and pendulous. The creature's head was carried so low that it appeared to have no neck. Dark reddish-black hair covered its body, except for parts of the face, the palms, and the soles of its feet. The two men estimated that the creature was at least seven feet tall and must have weighed between 350 and 450 pounds. Patterson quickly took a 16mm movie camera, loaded with color film, from his saddlebag and started filming the creature.

### Pursuing the creature

At first, he filmed at a distance of about 110 feet. Then, as he ran in pursuit, he closed to about 80 feet away. As the beast started to walk across the sandy spur of the creek, Patterson stopped running. The creature turned and looked at him, then disappeared into the dense woods.

### Large footprints

The men believed that they had encountered a Bigfoot, one of the legendary race of hairy primates that allegedly have been sighted for centuries, and that are still believed to inhabit the forests of the Pacific Northwest. The creature is known as Bigfoot in the United States because of its large footprints. In Canada, where it is claimed, a similar creature is often sighted, it is known as the Sasquatch, a Salish Indian name.

Patterson and Gimlin were longtime believers in the existence of Bigfoot.

> # Prof. Grover S. Krantz pointed out that the creature did not seem to walk like a human being.

*Bigfoot on film*
*The film of an alleged Bigfoot showed no clear evidence that the creature was a fake.*

They had ridden into this densely forested region, where Bigfoots had often been spotted, expressly to see if they could track and film one, in order to make a documentary on Bigfoot. They had been traveling on horseback for several days through the Bluff Creek area, filming the scenic terrain. After the creature vanished into the woods, Patterson filmed the footprints and made casts of the tracks. These casts showed prints that were $14^1/_2$ inches long and 5 inches wide. The distance between each stride was roughly 40 inches. Patterson shot only 24 feet of film. It was jumpy and hard to follow, and ran for only a minute or two. Scientists who examined the film saw no clear reason to dismiss it as a fake. But the majority believed that the subject filmed must have been a man dressed in a fur suit.

### Walks like a man?

In 1991 anthropologist Prof. Grover S. Krantz, of Washington State University, analyzed the film and pointed out that the creature did not walk like a human being: It appeared to maintain foot contact with the ground for a longer period. As the creature placed one foot on the ground, it straightened that leg fully. But then, as the body passed over this supporting limb, the leg was bent. On the next stride, the leg was extended fully back, then the leg was bent, with the knee swung far forward and the foot lifted high off the ground.

Prof. Krantz came to the conclusion that the size and the muscular development of the creature on the film were much greater than that considered possible in a human being.

Such creatures have been sighted for centuries in the Pacific Northwest, from British Columbia down to northern California, and east through the Rocky Mountains. The American Indians incorporated Bigfoot stories into their legends. Pioneers allegedly encountered Bigfoot and saw its tracks. In 1811, for example, a Canadian trader, David Thompson, crossing the northern Rocky Mountains, near what is now Jasper, Alberta, reportedly saw huge tracks measuring 14 inches long and 8 inches wide imprinted in the snow.

## Centuries of sightings

There have been thousands of sightings of Bigfoot and Sasquatch in North America since the 1950's. One particular sighting that excited Bigfoot investigators took place on June 10, 1982, in the Walla Walla area of the Umatilla National Forest in Washington State. Forest patrolman Paul Freeman was walking up an old logging spur, tracking a herd

of elk, when he suddenly saw something step off a bank on to the road below him at a distance of about 65 yards.

Freeman claimed the creature looked exactly like pictures he had seen of prehistoric man. It was covered with thick reddish-brown hair, but on its face and chest the hair was thin enough to reveal skin the color of dark brown leather. The creature stood about 8 1/2 feet tall and looked heavy. Freeman was certain that

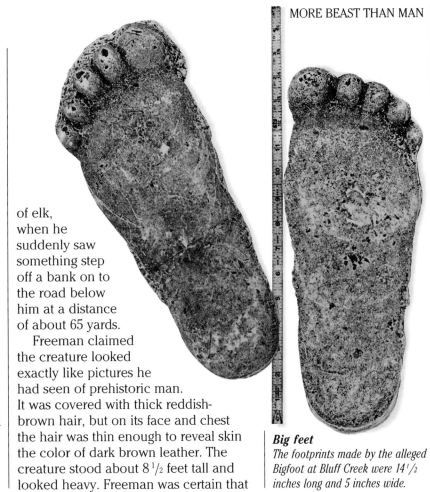

**Big feet**
*The footprints made by the alleged Bigfoot at Bluff Creek were 14 1/2 inches long and 5 inches wide.*

---

**GIANT AMONG PRIMATES**

A giant ape named *Gigantopithecus* is believed to have lived in China until 500,000–300,000 years ago. In the last 50 years three fossilized lower jaws and more than a thousand loose teeth thought to belong to the animal have been found.

From these remains anthropologists have been able to construct a picture of the giant primate. The teeth suggest a creature neither fully human nor fully ape. The jaws are much larger than those of male gorillas, who typically weigh 400 pounds, and they have led experts to theorize that the giant ape's weight might have been double that of a gorilla. The differing jaws of what appear to be male and female specimens suggest that the former weighed around 800 pounds and the latter around 500 pounds. If these estimates are correct, they indicate that *Gigantopithecus* was probably the largest primate that ever lived.

**Walking on two legs**
The jaws are extremely wide. Anthropologist Prof. Grover S. Krantz

*Prof. Krantz with the cast of a track left by a Bigfoot*

believes that the most likely reason for this is that the jaws had to accommodate the animal's neck, which, it is believed, was carried between, rather than behind, the rear corners of the jaws. The vertical orientation of the neck would imply that the entire body was carried in the upright position. *Gigantopithecus* therefore may well have stood and

walked in human fashion. It would probably have had an apelike face and its body would have been covered with hair. The relative scarcity of fossils suggests that these giant apes were rare and did not live in close social groups.

The earliest known *Gigantopithecus* jaw is from India and is estimated to be at least five million years old. Some fossils found in China date back about one million years. The most recently discovered fossil teeth (from northern Vietnam) are 300,000 years old. No remains dating from later than this have been found, and consequently most anthropologists believe that *Gigantopithecus* is extinct.

**Giant and hairy**
The description of *Gigantopithecus* is similar to that of giant hairy primates that have been spotted in remote regions of North America. Thus it is possible to speculate that, as with migrations of other mammals, some of these giant primates may have crossed a land bridge that existed between present-day Siberia and Alaska when the advancing glaciers of the last Ice Age, that occurred about 20,000–10,000 years ago, lowered the sea level.

It is even possible, if unlikely, that the descendants of these animals have survived in remote areas of North America and China.

***Strange encounter***
*Forest patrolman Paul Freeman holds the cast of a footprint of a Bigfoot he claimed to have seen in Umatilla National Forest, Washington State, in June 1982.*

**When Prof. Grover S. Krantz examined the casts he found that all showed unmistakable patches of dermal ridges — swirls of lines similar to fingerprints — under the toes and on the soles. These ridges occur only on the palms and soles of higher primates.**

it was not a bear, an animal with which he was very familiar. Nor did Freeman think it was someone dressed in a gorilla suit, because, he claimed, he could see muscles moving in its arms, legs, and shoulders. Freeman was soon joined by colleagues, who photographed and took casts of the tracks left by the creature. They found 21 footprints, each of which was 14 inches long and 7 inches wide, and six to eight feet apart.

When anthropologist Prof. Grover S. Krantz examined the casts he found that all showed unmistakable patches of dermal ridges — swirls of lines similar to fingerprints — under the toes and on the soles. These ridges occur only on the palms and soles of higher primates. Krantz believed that such dermal ridges would be extremely difficult for a hoaxer to incorporate into a fake print.

### Impressive evidence
Forty police fingerprint experts have studied the casts Freeman made, and most felt that they looked genuine. Yet when the casts were shown to anthropologists their opinions were mixed, with the majority saying that the prints were obviously faked. These experts suggested that the casts had been made from human footprints and had then been enlarged. This could have been done, they argued, by soaking a latex mold of a footprint in kerosene. The treatment would have uniformly expanded the mold by one half.

However, if the footprints had been enlarged in this way, the dermal ridge spacing on the prints would also have been increased. Yet all the fingerprint experts noted that the ridges on the casts were spaced as they would have been in casts of higher primates' feet.

### Solitary habits
Prof. Krantz believes that, by analyzing the eyewitness reports and physical traces, it is possible to construct a picture of how these giant hairy creatures might live.

He considers that they would be primarily vegetarians, solitary in their habits, and careful to avoid human contact. Some witnesses claim that they have observed Sasquatch either eating or carrying edible items, mostly vegetation. On some occasions the creatures are reported to consume meat. Krantz believes they might be more accurately described as opportunistic carnivores. This kind of diet would, in theory at least, fit in with the nutritional needs of mammals of this size in the North American forests.

### Nocturnal feeders
Half of the reported Bigfoot sightings occur at night. Krantz believes this behavior indicates that Bigfoots may be primarily nocturnal. This would also separate the feeding cycle between Bigfoots and bears, and thereby avoid direct conflict between large creatures over food sources: Bears forage by day.

Most sightings of Bigfoots or of their tracks concern lone creatures. Half of those who have spotted a Bigfoot report that the creature ran off when humans appeared — though not in panic. The other half describe an almost indifferent attitude toward the observer, with the Bigfoot moving off in a casual manner.

### The search for proof
Some accounts of Bigfoot are so detailed that they are hard to dismiss. Yet many of the Bigfoot and Sasquatch sightings may simply be of misidentified deer or bears. In addition, undoubtedly hoaxes have been perpetrated and footprints faked. It is only if some firm evidence were produced — such as skeletal material (even a single lower jawbone) — that scientists would be prepared to take seriously the existence of the elusive Bigfoot.

***Black bear track***
*The black bear's footprint is very different from alleged Bigfoot tracks.*

# ABDUCTED BY A SASQUATCH

## *Ostman saw his captors....They were four large, hairy creatures who looked at him with intense curiosity.*

WHILE ON VACATION IN 1924 in the mountains behind Toba Inlet on the coast of British Columbia, Canadian lumberman Albert Ostman's sleep was disturbed. As he lay in his sleeping bag, he suddenly had the sensation that he was being picked up. He soon realized that this was no dream. He found that he had been lifted up and carried off while trapped, and near suffocation, in his sleeping bag. He could not see his captor nor was he able to free himself. He was manhandled over rough terrain by his abductor for what he thought must have been about three hours.

### Terrifying journey

Ostman's terrifying, and uncomfortable, journey came to a sudden halt when he was abruptly dropped on the ground. The night was so dark that he could not see where he had been taken. He heard the clatter of pots and pans as what he thought to be his knapsack was tossed on the ground. Recovering himself, Ostman managed to extricate himself from his sleeping bag. He became aware that he was surrounded by some moving shapes that loomed large before him in the dark. He could not make out these creatures clearly but he could hear them chattering incomprehensibly among themselves.

When dawn broke, Ostman saw his captors for the first time. They were four large, hairy creatures who stood on two legs and looked at him with intense curiosity. The group was made up of the following: an adult male, about eight feet tall, that had apparently carried Ostman away; an adult female, about seven feet tall; a male that, at just over seven feet, looked full grown; and a young, smaller female.

The creatures had hair about six inches long on their heads while on the rest of their bodies the hair was short and thick. The only parts of their bodies that were not covered with hair were the palms of their hands, the soles of their feet, and the upper part of their noses and eyelids. They had large feet with padded soles. Except for the older female, they were, Ostman claimed, extremely agile.

### Trapped in a valley

Ostman found himself in a small valley that was enclosed by steep cliffs. Even though the creatures made no attempt to harm him, the adult male blocked the only exit from the valley and prevented Ostman from escaping. He was not harmed, and each day the young male offered him roots and grasses to eat. After five days of captivity, Ostman became desperate. The young male had sampled some snuff that the lumberman had in his knapsack. On the sixth morning, Ostman offered the tin containing the snuff to the adult male, which swallowed its whole contents in a single gulp. The creature immediately became ill and, during the ensuing confusion, Ostman finally managed to escape.

On Ostman's return to civilization, a local Indian told him that he had been abducted by a Sasquatch, a creature Ostman had never heard of before his experience. Anticipating that his story of the bizarre episode might be greeted with derision, Ostman kept it to himself for 33 years. Then, in 1957, he told it to Swiss-Canadian Bigfoot investigator René Dahinden.

# CREATURES FROM OUTER SPACE?

*Hairy monsters impervious to bullets, creatures emerging from spacecraft — are these the stuff of cryptozoology, science fiction, or fact?*

ON THE NIGHT OF MAY 13, 1977, the Sites family, who lived in Wantage, a remote and rural part of New Jersey, allegedly cornered a Bigfoot in their farmyard. The creature was enormous and hairy. It appeared to have no neck; its head rested squarely on its shoulders. On previous nights the same creature had reportedly killed many of the Sites's animals. The farmer took his shotgun and fired at the intruder with buckshot. Sites was certain that he had hit the creature but the Bigfoot appeared unaffected by the gunfire. Farm workers chased after the creature in a truck, but it made good its escape.

## Nonphysical beings

There is nothing in the majority of Bigfoot sightings to suggest that the witnesses saw anything other than a terrestrial creature, albeit of an unknown kind. Incidents such as the Wantage encounter can lead paranormal investigators to speculate that these creatures may be nonphysical beings visiting our planet from another dimension. A more down-to-earth explanation for the Bigfoot's invulnerability to gunfire may be that the ammunition was not powerful enough to bloody such a massive beast.

In the 1970's reports began to emerge that linked Bigfoot sightings directly with unidentified flying objects (UFO's). In October 1973, 15 people near Greensburg, Pennsylvania, saw a large red ball of light that appeared to descend onto distant pasture land. Three witnesses drove to the spot, where they claimed they saw a shining, dome-shaped spacecraft.

In the light that the strange craft gave off the witnesses said they saw two hairy, apelike creatures with green glowing eyes. One appeared to be about seven feet tall and the other even taller. As the creatures walked toward them the witnesses took fright, and one of the men fired three rounds from his rifle into the larger creature. As it was hit the creature made a whining sound and raised its hand toward its companion. The UFO disappeared and the creatures turned and slowly walked into nearby woods.

Some witnesses even claim to have looked inside spacecraft that were manned by Bigfoot-like creatures. In September 1989, near Tillamook,

## Witnesses claim to have looked inside spacecraft that were manned by Bigfoot-like creatures.

Oregon, a woman and her granddaughter saw a disk hovering just above the ground. As the woman approached to within 30 feet of it, a door opened and a humanlike being with blond hair and blue eyes, wearing a silver coverall, appeared. Behind a window next to the door the woman could see a Bigfoot-like creature, visible from the chest up. She stood transfixed by the appearance of the strange visitors until the spacecraft suddenly vanished.

### Geological stresses
These sightings remained very real to the eyewitnesses who experienced them. However, British paranormal researcher Janet Bord suggests that such UFO sightings and the strange qualities of these large apelike creatures may be somehow linked to electromagnetic energy fields in these locations generated by geological stresses deep within the earth. Bord believes this natural energy might cause anyone near it to experience strange phenomena.

# DE LOYS'S APE

*Apes, let alone ape-men, are not supposed to exist in South America. The alleged appearance of an ape-man in the rain forests of Colombia still puzzles scientists.*

**Dangerous journey**
*The journey through the dense tropical rain forest on the Venezuela-Colombia border proved hazardous for Dr. François de Loys and his team. Some members of the expedition were lost through disease and attacks by the hostile Motilone Indians.*

IN 1920 THE EMINENT SWISS GEOLOGIST Dr. François de Loys led a team of colleagues through the dense rain forests along the Tarra River on the Venezuela-Colombia border. While making their way through the treacherous forest one day, the foliage ahead of them parted, and two apelike creatures emerged from among the trees. They were about five feet tall and lacked tails. However, even more bizarre, they appeared to walk upright on their hind legs.

When the creatures saw the geologists, they became agitated, tearing off tree branches and rooting up surrounding vegetation as if in distress. The creatures moved forward, and the geologists, fearing they were about to be attacked, fired their guns at the one they believed to be the male. As they did so, he moved aside, and his companion received the hail of bullets and was killed. Seeing his companion fall to the ground, the male fled.

**Mystery ape**
*Only one photograph of the apelike creature that De Loys claimed to have found survived. The creature appears to have an almost humanlike expression.*

## A single photograph
The geologists examined the carcass. The apelike creature proved to be female. They sat her on a gasoline crate and, using a pole tucked under her chin to prop her body in an upright position, photographed her. It had become immediately apparent that it would be impossible to transport the creature's already decomposing body through the humid rain forests, and so they left the carcass behind. Later, on their journey down river, their boat capsized. And only one photograph survived.

**Gorilla-like carving**

## Heated dispute
This photograph provoked one of the most heated disputes in modern-day zoology. On his return to Europe, De Loys showed the photograph to the eminent French anthropologist Prof. George Montandon, who was convinced that its subject represented a major zoological discovery. He duly christened it *Ameranthropoides loysi* ("Loys's American ape") in a scientific paper in May 1929.

Other scientists, however, remained unconvinced about Montandon's claim. They believed that in overall appearance, De Loys's ape resembled a robust spider monkey. Yet there was no known spider monkey that had ever attained a height of 5 feet 1 inch (the measurement recorded by De Loys). The creature's limbs also seemed stockier, and its thorax was longer and flatter than would be expected. Its teeth numbered 32, whereas most South American primates have at least 36.

## Without a tail

The absence of a tail appeared to indicate that the creature was not a spider monkey. Yet some investigators suspected that a hoax was involved and that the tail had been deliberately cut off or hidden from view in the photograph. They argued that the creature had been modified to appear larger and more distinctive than it really was.

In response to these detractors, Montandon published further papers in which he painstakingly discussed the anatomical significance of *Ameranthropoides* in order to refute such speculation. By obtaining and measuring crates identical to the one supporting the creature in the photograph, he showed that *Ameranthropoides* was indeed just over five feet tall. This demonstration confirmed De Loys's measurements. Yet despite all Montandon's strenuous efforts, his critics remained adamant — the creature was not an ape. Eventually the debate was forgotten.

## Failed fraud

However, every so often, zoologists revive the De Loys case. Some support Montandon; others condemn the incident as a failed fraud. The American cryptozoologist Ivan T. Sanderson argued that it was a spider monkey carcass that appeared robust merely because its body was swollen by an accumulation of gas due to putrefaction. He added that its tailless state was artificial, not natural.

## Circumstantial evidence

The British zoologist Dr. Karl P. N. Shuker believes that there is circumstantial evidence that adds weight to the possibility that the creature De Loys photographed might exist. From earliest times, Dr. Shuker points out, Indian tribes inhabiting the jungles of South America have believed in the existence of apelike creatures that walk on two legs and do not have tails. The names of these creatures vary from country to country — from *mapinguary* (in Brazil and Bolivia) and *didi* (Guyana), to *vasitri* (Venezuela), and *shiru* (Colombia) — but their appearance is reportedly much the same.

Among the crumbling remains of various ancient South American, and also Mexican, cities are sculptures of remarkable gorilla-like beasts. These stone carvings appear to resemble the controversial South American ape-man.

Dr. Shuker suggests that the answer to the riddle of the identity of De Loys's ape may still remain hidden in the depths of South America's vast and near-impenetrable rain forests.

> From earliest times, Indian tribes inhabiting the jungles of South America have believed in the existence of apelike creatures that walk on two legs and do not have tails.

*Venezuela and Colombia*
*The South American ape-man was allegedly seen on the border of Venezuela and Colombia. These countries in the northwest of South America are shown in red on the map.*

*Temperamental monkey*
*Spider monkeys are found in the South American rain forests, from Mexico to Brazil. Spider monkeys are known to display the same agitated behavior shown by the creatures De Loys encountered.*

# THE YETI

**A number of reliable witnesses have reported seeing a mysterious man-beast, known as the Yeti, on the snowy slopes of the Himalayas. Is it possible that such a creature really exists?**

*I*N SEPTEMBER 1921, Lt. Col. C. K. Howard-Bury, of the British Army, neared Lhapka-La Pass, northern Tibet, at 17,000 feet above sea level, during an attempt to climb the north face of Mount Everest, the world's highest mountain. As he looked through his binoculars, he saw dark forms moving about on a snowfield above him. Some days later, Howard-Bury reached the location, at 23,000 feet, where he had seen these mysterious figures. There he found to his great astonishment that some creature had left giant humanlike footprints in the snow.

### "Abominable Snowman"

When reports of these tracks reached the Western world, they immediately captured the public's imagination. Local Sherpa guides called the creature *metoh-kangmi,* which was mistakenly translated by Howard-Bury's superiors in India, to whom he reported the incident, as the "Abominable Snowman." The word the Sherpas used was in fact the generic term for a number of mysterious creatures that they believed roamed across the snowfields. This report began the modern myth of the Himalayan man-beast.

In November 1951, British mountaineers Eric Shipton and Michael Ward were making their way over the southwestern slopes of the Menlung glacier in the Himalayas, at 20,000 feet above sea level, when they came upon giant tracks in the snow. They followed these tracks for about a mile and came to a spot where the ice was thin. Here they found a giant footprint that measured 13 inches long and 8 inches wide. Shipton saw that the imprint had been made recently because it had not had time to melt. Using Ward's ice ax to show scale, Shipton photographed the footprint of what appeared to be a five-toed anthropoid creature.

### "That-there thing"

The Sherpas who acted as Shipton's mountain guides had no difficulty in identifying the creatures that had left these tracks. To them they were Yetis, wild creatures of the mountains. (The word *Yeti* comes from the Sherpa term *yeh-teh* meaning "that-there thing.")

Nepal and Tibet have a long history of sightings of these mysterious creatures. Investigations into Yeti sightings and the analysis of alleged footprints have persuaded cryptozoologists that the Himalayas may conceal some as yet unknown primate. From eyewitness reports and analysis of footprints, cryptozoologist Ivan T. Sanderson built up a picture of three forms of Yeti.

## Manlike being

The *teh-lma* ("manlike being") is known as the little Yeti. It is believed to stand about three or four feet tall. Such creatures appear to inhabit the warm valleys where they are believed to eat frogs and insects. They have thick red fur and a slight mane. Their feet create distinctive five-inch-long footprints. The second form, the *meh-teh* (the "man-

> **They followed the tracks and came to a spot where the ice was thin. Here they found a giant footprint that measured 13 inches long and 8 inches wide.**

beast") has a conical head, stout neck, and a wide mouth with no lips. It is reportedly man-size and covered in reddish-brown thick fur. It supposedly eats a wide variety of small animals, birds, and plants. Its five-toed feet are short and very broad, with a second toe longer than the big toe. This form of Yeti is supposedly shy and retiring and tends to stay in the upper mountain forests. (American cryptozoologist Loren Coleman believes that it is the sight of a *meh-teh* venturing across snowfields that has caused the furor associated with sightings of the Abominable Snowman.)

## "The hulking living thing"

The third form of Yeti, the *dzu-teh* ("the hulking living thing"), is often overlooked because people who allegedly encounter this creature believe that they may have seen a large red bear rather than a Yeti. Sanderson's researches led him to believe that the *dzu-teh* is a much taller and bulkier creature than the *meh-teh*. It has a long, dark, shaggy coat, a flat head, and a beetling brow. It has long, powerful arms and huge hands, and very humanlike feet that leave imprints like those of a giant man. The French crypto-zoologist Dr. Bernard Heuvelmans suggested that the *dzu-teh* might be a descendant of, or related to, *Gigantopithecus*, the largest primate known, a creature believed to have become extinct 300,000 years ago.

### Seeking the Yeti

After the publication of Shipton's photograph of alleged Yeti footprints in 1951, many expeditions attempted to discover the Yeti. In 1957 the Texas oil millionaire and cryptozoologist Tom Slick investigated reports of apelike men in Nepal.

*A Yeti footprint?*

During Slick's first expedition to Nepal in 1957, he discovered 15 eyewitnesses who claimed to have seen the Yeti. Showing photographs of 20 animals that might be confused with Yetis — including a bear, a langur monkey, and a orangutan — Slick asked the local people to identify what they had seen.

### Unanimous selection

Slick wrote in his journal at the time: "We asked these people to select the photographs that most resemble the Yeti. It was quite impressive that there was a unanimous selection, in the same order, with the first choice being the gorilla standing up, the second choice being a drawing of a prehistoric ape-man, *Australopithecus*, and the third choice being an orangutan standing up, which they liked particularly for the long hair." Anthropologists at the British

> **During his expedition, Slick discovered 15 eyewitnesses who claimed to have seen the Yeti.**

***Treasured skullcap***
*A monk at the Pangboche monastery in Nepal wearing a skullcap allegedly made from Yeti skin. These skullcaps are regarded as sacred relics by their Buddhist guardians.*

Museum in London had suggested that Yetis were simply bears or langur monkeys that had been misidentified. Nevertheless each time Slick showed a photograph of a bear or a monkey, the eyewitnesses would state matter-of-factly, that this was a bear, not a Yeti, or this was a monkey, not a Yeti.

### Physical evidence

In 1959 another expedition to Nepal led by Slick discovered alleged Yeti droppings. After analysis these were found to contain a previously unknown parasitic worm. This was an important find for cryptozoologists. As Dr. Bernard Heuvelmans observed: "Since each species of mammal has its own parasites, this indicated that the host animal is also equally an unknown animal."

There are other examples of alleged physical remains of Yetis. Slick first heard

**Seeking the Yeti**
*The Texas millionaire and cryptozoologist Tom Slick mounted three expeditions to the Himalayas to seach for evidence of the Yeti.*

come to light in 1958. Slick was shown what was alleged to be a Yeti's hand at the Buddhist monastery at Pangboche, Nepal. Photographs of the hand were presented to the British primatologist Prof. W. C. Osman-Hill of the Zoological Society of London. His opinion was that the hand might have come from an unknown anthropoid.

Sections of the Pangboche hand were smuggled out of Nepal by Peter Byrne, a member of Slick's expedition in 1959. The thumb, a section of the index finger, and a piece of wizened and darkened skin from the hand were given to Prof. Osman-Hill for analysis. After performing tests on the skin sample, Prof. Osman-Hill concluded the tissues did not come from a human or known primate.

### Unknown primate

It appears that some pieces of the Pangboche hand had also been sent to an American anthropologist, Dr. George Agogino, at the University of Wyoming. No results of his analysis, however, were ever published. Then, in 1992, the American television program *Unsolved Mysteries* sought out Dr. Agogino, who still had the samples. After more than 30 years, his samples were analyzed.

On February 12, 1992, the broadcast revealed that analysis at the biomedical laboratories of the University of California, at Los Angeles, had shown that the skin was close to being human but was not. But further research into the Pangboche hand became impossible. Thieves had broken into the Pangboche monastery in May 1991 and stolen the rest of the Pangboche hand and an alleged Yeti skullcap also kept there.

### Compelling tales

Eyewitnesses who claim to have seen the Yeti often tell compelling tales. There is undoubtedly some evidence, however controversial, of an unknown creature living in the snows of Tibet and Nepal. But until concrete evidence appears, such as fossil remains or a carcass, the Yeti's existence remains unproven.

**Mystery hand**
*Scientific analysis of the alleged Yeti hand from the Pangboche monastery, Nepal, suggested that it may belong to some unknown primate.*

After performing tests on the skin sample, Prof. Osman-Hill concluded the tissues did not come from a human or known primate.

in the late 1950's reports of skullcaps made from Yeti skin. It was not until 1960, however, that these Yeti skullcaps were actually seen by Western investigators, when the New Zealand mountaineer Sir Edmund Hillary, the conquerer of Mount Everest, led a three-month expedition to Nepal to gather information on the Yeti.

At the Buddhist temple at Khumjung he was shown one of these skullcaps. The chief lama allowed Hillary to take the skullcap away for scientific analysis. But scientists established that the skin did not come from an unknown anthropoid but from a rare Himalayan creature called the serow, a goat-like beast that is a member of the goat-antelope family.

A different piece of evidence that might support the existence of an unknown primate in the Himalayas had

# NEANDERTHAL SURVIVORS?

***Is it possible that a race of early humans still survives in the remote mountain ranges of central Asia?***

IN AUGUST 1991 IN THE Caucasus Mountains in the republic of Kazakhstan, central Asia, the Russian scientist Gregori Patchenkoff claimed that he had encountered, and observed for six minutes, a strange apelike creature. This large primate walked upright. The creature was between 5 feet 8 inches and 6 feet tall, and its body was covered with long reddish fur. Its face was not human, but it was not entirely apelike. It reminded Patchenkoff of a prehistoric man. He believed that he had seen a creature known as an Alma.

### Familiar creatures

In the Caucasus, Almas are well known by the local people, who tell numerous stories of an apparent familiarity between humans and these creatures. Eyewitness accounts dating back a hundred years describe Almas communicating with humans by means of gestures. There were even stories of Almas bartering food for trinkets. In 1964 the Soviet scientist Boris Porshnev obtained some astonishing first-hand accounts from people who said that they clearly remembered, as small children, a female Alma called Zana who had been captured in the forests of Mount Zaadan in the Caucasus and held in captivity in a local village. They said that her skin was grayish black and that she was covered in reddish hair. She was said to communicate using sounds but never learned to speak. Zana was described as having a large face with a jutting jaw, high cheekbones, and a fierce expression. She became pregnant and eventually, so the story goes, produced four children. Zana died in the 1880's. In 1964 her descendants were reportedly still living in the region. During his research, Porshnev was even able to visit two adults who were claimed to be Zana's grandchildren.

The witnesses Porshnev spoke to claimed that Zana's offspring differed only slightly from other children. Their appearance was reportedly quite human except for an unusual swarthiness. The villagers claimed that

*Alma offspring?*
*The Soviet scientist Igor Bourtsev holds a skull claimed to be that of the son of a human male and an Alma female known as Zana.*

## The appearance of Zana's offspring was reportedly quite human except for an unusual swarthiness.

Zana's children had learned to speak. One of her grandchildren was said to be an accomplished mimic of animal sounds. All of her offspring were also alleged to be extremely physically strong.

When reported sightings of wild, hairy, upright-walking creatures first came to public attention, some researchers suggested that they might be Neanderthals. These ancient ancestors of modern man were thought

*Alma-like skull?*
*This skull of a Neanderthal has the heavy brow and high cheekbones described by people who claim to have seen Almas.*

***Republic of Kazakhstan***
*Almas, creatures allegedly resembling Neanderthal man, have been reported in the central Asian republic of Kazakhstan, shown here in red as part of the former U.S.S.R.*

Dr. Kofman has studied Almas for 30 years. She believes Almas are nomadic, omnivorous, and shy creatures, living in the mountains at heights of 8,000 to 12,000 feet, from which they sometimes descend to raid crops. She has collected more than 500 eyewitness accounts. These include descriptions of Alma families, including children. However, footprints, droppings, hairs, and stories are all Dr. Kofman has, thus far, to show for her work.

to have become extinct about 30,000 years ago, but it was rumored that they may have survived in remote areas.

The descriptions of the Almas' faces resemble those of Neanderthals. Other characteristics attributed to Almas, such as communicating through gestures and making stone tools, might also tie in with behavior expected of a Neanderthal.

## Searching for the Almas
In 1992 the Russian scientist Dr. Marie-Jeanne Kofman headed a team of French and Soviet scientists attempting to confirm the existence of Almas.

***Recognizable being***
*Fossil remains indicate that Neanderthal man may have looked somewhat similar to people today. This model, at the Field Museum in Chicago, was reconstructed using Neanderthal bones as a guide.*

***Alma terrain***
*Almas are said to dwell in the sparsely populated, mountainous region of the Caucasus, in central Asia.*

# THE APE-MEN OF SUMATRA

*The island of Sumatra reportedly conceals a strange, apelike creature called the orang pendek. Local folklore tells how this creature is said to walk with backward-pointing feet.*

IN OCTOBER 1923 A DUTCH SETTLER named Van Herwaarden was traveling through dense forest near the village of Pangkalan Balai, in the Banjoeasin district on the island of Sumatra, in the Dutch East Indies, which is present-day Indonesia. Suddenly he saw a slight movement in the foliage ahead of him. He moved forward, slowly, with his hunting rifle at the ready. On a branch, 10 feet above the ground, he saw what appeared to him at first sight to be some type of ape.

### Mysterious animal

Van Herwaarden was close enough to see that this dark, hairy creature was unlike any ape he had seen before. He stared at the mysterious figure. It appeared to be about five feet tall. It had a thick head of hair, which fell below its shoulders. Its short feet resembled

> ## Van Herwaarden was struck by the almost humanlike expression in the creature's eyes and its smooth, hairless brown face. It appeared to be more like a person than an animal.

those of a child. Van Herwaarden was immediately struck by the almost humanlike expression in the creature's eyes and its smooth, hairless brown face. It appeared to be more like a person than an animal.

Pressing itself tightly against the trunk of a tree in an attempt to make itself inconspicuous, the creature made a plaintive *"hu-hu"* call. To the Dutch settler's astonishment the cry was answered by similar sounds echoing from the forest nearby.

Excited at his extraordinary find, the Dutchman climbed the tree, readying himself to catch hold of the creature. But the odd figure suddenly swung itself to the ground and began to run away. Van Herwaarden panicked — in another moment the creature would be gone for good. And without any physical evidence of its

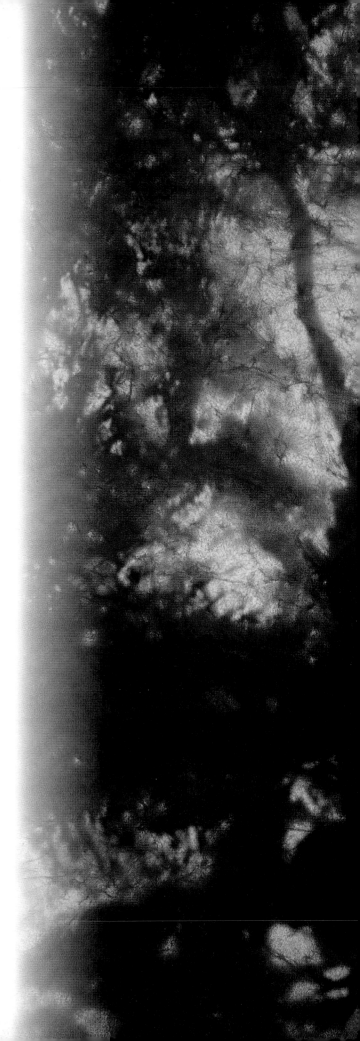

**Upright bear**
*The Malayan sun bear often adopts a vertical posture. Its footprints look like those of a small broad-footed human.*

existence, he knew that no one would believe his claim that he had just seen an ape-man in the forest. He reached for his gun and took aim. Then he stopped. As he recalled later: "Many people may think me childish if I say that when I saw its flying hair in the sights I did not pull the trigger. I suddenly felt that I was going to commit murder."

### Little man of Sumatra

Van Herwaarden had apparently encountered the *orang pendek,* or "little man," a creature well known to the people of Sumatra. His account constitutes the most detailed sighting of the apelike creature, which is said to live there in the forests of the Barisan Mountains.

In 1917, six years before Van Herwaarden's encounter, another Dutchman, named Oostingh, the manager of a coffee plantation at Dataran, was wandering through the forest, lost in the eastern foothills of Bukit Kaba. His spirits rose when he thought he caught sight of someone, apparently in the act of building a fire. However, as he approached, he realized that this figure was neither clothed, nor entirely human. The strange creature backed away several paces from Oostingh and then swung off through the trees. Oostingh was convinced it was not an orangutan. He described it as resembling "a monstrously large siamang" but with extremely short hair. (The siamang is the world's largest species of gibbon, and has long hair.)

After the publication of Oostingh's account, other European witnesses began to come forward and tell of their encounters with *orang pendeks.* Some eyewitnesses gave first-hand descriptions of the creature; others made sketches of footprints, and some even claimed to have samples of hair. Most zoologists, however, suggested that the creature these people had seen was a known mammal, such as an orangutan.

Others argued that the creature might be a relict ancestor of man. Zoologists who pursued this theory pointed to the

> ## "In this kingdom are found men with tails, a span in length, like those of a dog, but not covered with hair."
>
> **Marco Polo**

fact that in 1894 the Dutch geologist Dr. Eugène Dubois had discovered the remains of an ape-man, an early hominid he called *Pithecanthropus erectus,* on the neighboring island of Java.

### Men with tails

Yet sightings of *orang pendeks* have been reported for centuries on Sumatra. When the 13th-century Venetian traveler Marco Polo visited Sumatra on his journey back to Venice from China, he gave this description of the creature: "In this kingdom are found men with tails, a span in length, like those of a dog, but not covered with hair."

**Island hunter**
*On Siberut, an island off western Sumatra, the islanders often claim they have seen the* orang pendek.

According to the Kubu, an indigenous tribe of the island's interior, these ape-men did not have tails. The same creatures were also known variously as the *orang letjo*, meaning "gibbering man" — or by the names *sedapa* or *gugu*. Local folktales told how these creatures walked with backward-pointing feet to confuse anyone bold enough to try to track them. The Kubu tribespeople also maintained that unless tobacco was left for them at night, the creatures would go on the rampage, screaming as they tore up the natives' camp.

**Upright gibbon**
*The siamang is a species of gibbon found on Sumatra. It is known to walk on two feet.*

### Charming folklore
Until the beginning of the 20th century, Western visitors to Sumatra paid little attention to the native accounts of the *orang pendek*. With no corroborative sightings from Europeans, they were considered part of the island's rather charming folklore.

Then in 1924 Dr. K. W. Dammerman, curator of the Buitenzorg Museum, on the neighboring island of Java, received a paraffin-wax mold of a footprint that was supposed to be that of an *orang pendek*. However, after examining it carefully, Dr. Dammerman concluded that the impression was that of the flat hind foot of a Malayan sun bear. He noted that this species habitually stood on two legs. Its claws were often retracted; this might explain why they did not show in prints.

### Back-to-front feet
Dr. Dammerman also concluded that some smaller footprints discovered in the same place were not of young *orang*

> **Folktales told how *orang pendeks* walked with backward-pointing feet to confuse anyone audacious enough to try to track them.**

*pendeks* as some had suggested. Although the sun bear stands on its hind legs, it goes down on all fours to walk, creating tracks that are a smudged amalgam of front and hind feet.

### Standing bear
This identification possibly explained the old folklore belief that the *orang pendek* actually walked with its feet turned back-to-front. This idea might have originated in the sun bear's tendency of standing with its toes turned inward.

In May 1932, it looked as if the mystery of the *orang pendek* might be solved. Four Kubu tribesmen brought in what they claimed was the body of an *orang pendek*. However, it all turned out to be a hoax. The locals had sharpened the teeth, stretched the nose, and shaved the fur of a type of leaf-eating monkey known as the langur.

### The search continues
Cryptozoologists have not abandoned the search for the *orang pendek*. In July 1989 the British investigator Deborah Martyr arrived in Sumatra to investigate the animal. Martyr was led by local people to a forest area around Mount Kerinci. There she discovered a fresh set of tracks that were attributed by the locals to the *orang pendek*. But one of the two casts that Martyr made was broken in transit. The other was sent to the National Park in Sumatra, where it was later lost.

Martyr still believes that an unknown primate may possibly exist today in the Barisan Mountains. Investigations are still continuing in Sumatra to establish the true identity of the *orang pendek*.

*Java man*
*Dr. Eugène Dubois made this reconstruction of an ape-man, known as* Pithecanthropus erectus, *based on the remains he discovered on the island of Java, Indonesia.*

# AFRICAN MAN-BEASTS

**An astonishing range of mysterious man-beasts continue to be reported in the continent of Africa.**

*I*N FEBRUARY 1976 APE-MAN OLIVER, a bald, freckled chimpanzee who stood some 4¹/₂ feet tall and walked upright, was presented to the public at a news conference in New York City. Ape-man Oliver had supposedly been caught in Zaire, Central Africa, by a South African animal trainer, Frank Burgler, who sold the unusual chimpanzee to a New York attorney, Michael Miller, for $10,000.

### Mutant chimpanzee

Ape-man Oliver caused much interest among zoologists. Some suggested that he might be a crossbreed between a chimpanzee and a mystery man-beast reported in East Africa, called the *agogwe*. Others argued that Oliver was a mutant chimpanzee with one less chromosome than normal. British zoologist Dr. Karl P. N. Shuker believes Oliver was almost certainly nothing more than an elderly specimen of West African chimpanzee showing typical signs of baldness and freckled skin.

Physical evidence, however, has proved that mystery apes could exist in Africa. One such creature is the pygmy gorilla. Skeletons and skins obtained over a century ago in what is now Gabon, West Africa, indicate that this species grew no taller

***Ghostly chimpanzee***
*In March 1964 Ufiti, a chimpanzee with gorilla-like features, was captured in southeast Africa and sent to Chester Zoo in England. Its name, Ufiti, means "ghost."*

> ## Ape-man Oliver caused much interest among zoologists. Some suggested that he might be a crossbreed between a chimpanzee and a mystery man-beast reported in East Africa, called the *agogwe*.

than 4¹/₂ feet. (Mountain and lowland gorillas usually attain a height of 6 feet.) While many zoologists deny that these remains are of any significance, crypto-zoologist Dr. Bernard Heuvelmans believes that they might support the existence of an otherwise unknown dwarf race of gorilla.

A strange female gorilla-like chimpanzee was captured on the Loango coast of what is now the Congo Republic, in 1874. Named Mafuca, she was brought to Dresden Zoo. Most zoologists consider Mafuca to be, at most, a subspecies of the common chimpanzee. A

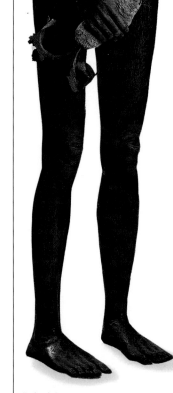

***Primitive woman***
*This model of an adult female australopithecine was reconstructed from remains found at Sterkfontein, South Africa.*

Mafuca-like chimpanzee is also reported in Gabon, West Africa, where it is called the *koolookamba*. Although crypto-zoologists have been intrigued by native claims that it is a hybrid of chimpanzee and gorilla, no such hybrid has ever been identified.

In 1959 another curious chimpanzee, with gorilla-like features, was sighted in the forests of Nkata Bay, in what is now Malawi, southeast Africa, several hundred miles from the nearest known chimpanzee colony. Referred to locally as Ufiti (meaning "ghost"), the creature was captured and sent in 1964 to Chester Zoo, in central England.

## Slender and robust remains
The most primitive African hominids presently known from fossils belong to the genus *Australopithecus*, which first appeared more than 3 million years ago.

**Dwarf gorilla**
*A model of a pygmy gorilla with her young, reconstructed on the basis of bones and skins supplied by hunters.*

Geologists have found remains of two forms of australopithecines which indicate that both slender and robust types existed. Cryptozoologists believe that some of the mystery apes reported in Africa may be modern-day representatives of these creatures.

Some reports of some mysterious man-beasts may possibly describe survivors of the species of slender australopithecines.

One such creature, the *agogwe*, reported in Tanzania, East Africa, is said to be a small, russet-furred, manlike being. It is sometimes described as mixing freely with other primates such as baboons.

## Quaint myth
The same creature is reported in Senegal, West Africa, where it is known as the *fating'ho*. Although deemed nothing more than a quaint myth by the younger generation of Senegal's Mandinka tribe, the wildlife enthusiast Owen Burnham, who has lived in Senegal for many years, reported that the elderly Mandinkas freely speak of the *fating'ho* as being as real as any of the known animals inhabiting Senegal.

Other man-beasts that have been sighted resemble reconstructions made of the more robust australopithecines. These include the *kikomba* of Zaire, and Sudan's *wa'ab*. Cryptozoologists also suggest that these beasts might even be related to *Homo erectus*.

## Unknown creatures
During the 20th century many previously unknown creatures — such as the mountain gorilla and the pygmy chimpanzee — have been discovered on the continent of Africa. But physical evidence is still needed to establish the existence of a range of reported African man-beasts.

**Zaire, central Africa**
*The mystery primate known as Ape-man Oliver was caught in Zaire.*

**Human relative**
*This australopithecine skull was found in Sterkfontein, South Africa. The skull indicates that it had a rather apelike head, with a low forehead and a flat nose.*

# CHAPTER FOUR

# MAN INTO BEAST

*The bloodsucking vampire that stalks its victims in the night, the flesh-eating werewolf...such terrifying transformations of man into beast have been recorded since earliest times. Equally amazing but less nightmarish metamorphoses have also been reported.*

In the early hours of a gray August morning in 1727, a group of men entered the cemetery in the village of Meduegya, Serbia. The men made their way toward the spot where the sexton was already hard at work digging up a recent grave. Before long a wooden coffin was exposed, and this was dragged roughly up out of the ground.

When the lid was prized off, a young boy who had accompanied the men fainted away. When the investigators probed the remains, the skin came loose to reveal a

**Romanian devil**
*The Romanian warrior-prince Vlad IV was said to have ordered the torture and execution of thousands of people. A statue of Vlad stands today in Tîrgoviste, which was once the capital of Walachia, a region in southern Romania over which he ruled in the mid-15th century.*

new skin that had formed beneath the old. The beard and the nails of the corpse had grown visibly. The dead body's mouth was wide open and fresh blood had trickled down from one corner. "So, you have not wiped your mouth since last night's work," the sexton is reported to have cried.

### Piercing scream
The men scattered garlic over the corpse and drove a sharp stake through its chest. Allegedly, a piercing scream was heard and a jet of blood gushed up around the stake. Then the men decapitated the corpse.

To their way of thinking, the men of Meduegya who carried out these macabre and bloody actions had good reason to do so. For they believed that the exhumed man, a local farmer named Arnold Paole, was a vampire, one of the most feared of all human transformations — a creature of the living dead who feeds off the blood of live animals and humans.

### Attacked by a vampire
While serving as a soldier in Greece near the border of Serbia, which was ruled by Turkey at that time, Paole claimed he had been attacked and bitten by a vampire. As a result — according to folk beliefs then widespread in central and eastern Europe — Paole was doomed to become a vampire when he died.

Several months after his death, so the story goes, villagers claimed that they had seen Paole at night. Some people complained that they had been haunted by him and had felt weak and ill as a result. Such was the hysteria among the villagers that they were convinced that Paole, who had been a well-respected member of the community, had indeed become a vampire.

When four people died suddenly, the villagers panicked. They petitioned the district governor to exhume Paole's body. They also apparently exhumed the other four bodies, and then drove stakes through their hearts. All five bodies were cremated and their ashes scattered. Only then, according to the various accounts, did the people of Meduegya feel safe.

### The vampires return
However, five years later panic again returned to the village. Within the space of several months, 17 people reportedly died of severe anemia, thought to be the classic symptom of having been attacked by a vampire. Such was the hysteria surrounding this case that in January 1732 a royal commission, known as the Deputation of Belgrade, was set up by Duke Charles Alexander of Württemberg to investigate the deaths in Meduegya. Paole, it was claimed, had sucked

> **The dead body's mouth was wide open and fresh blood trickled down from one corner. "So, you have not wiped your mouth since last night's work," the sexton reportedly cried.**

blood from cattle that were eaten by the villagers, who then supposedly became vampires. The corpses were exhumed, and many were found to show no signs of decomposition, another apparent indication of vampirism. The findings of the commission were that the deaths in Meduegya were the result of vampirism.

### Witches and wizards
The word vampire is derived from a Russian word for witch, and from ancient times a connection was thought to exist between the two: Witches, wizards, heretics, and evildoers were believed to be transformed at death into vampires. During the Salem witch trials that took place in Massachusetts in 1692, charges of vampirism were brought against many of the accused.

Suicide victims, too, were believed to become vampires. And the belief in vampires was so strong in England that it was not until 1823 that a law was passed that kept people from driving a stake through the hearts of suicide victims to prevent them from turning into vampires. The reason behind this practice was the belief that the stake would prevent the tormented soul from rising out of the grave and terrorizing the community.

Other precautions taken to prevent the dead from turning into bloodsucking vampires were to place corpses face down in the coffin, to decapitate them, or to put garlic in their mouths.

## A continuing horror

So ingrained were many of these beliefs that accounts of vampirism are still reported in modern times. In 1939, in Romania, investigators interviewed a peasant woman named Tinka, who claimed her father was a vampire. The day after he was laid out for burial, villagers discovered that his face was still flushed and his body was supple. The man was quickly branded a vampire, and a stake was driven through his heart.

In 1973, in the English industrial town of Stoke on Trent, a Polish immigrant, Demetrious Myicura, was found choked to death on a clove of garlic. The coroner's inquest found that Myicura had been so terrified of being attacked by vampires that he had placed garlic in his mouth as protection. His room was strewn with salt, another traditional form of protection against vampire attacks.

## Premature burial

The bizarre but compelling legends of vampires may have their origins in the phenomenon of premature burial. Before modern medical techniques and procedures, there were numerous cases of people being buried while still alive. Such victims may have suffered from a condition known as catalepsy (a trance-like state when all signs of life appear to be absent). Thus, if the grave of a victim of premature burial were

*Torturer's chapel*
*In Tirgoviste local legend tells how, after watching his victims being tortured, Vlad would go to the castle's chapel to pray.*

*Castle of blood*
*Many of the sadistic acts of the notorious Vlad Tepes (meaning "Impaler") took place at his castle in Tirgoviste, southern Romania.*

### COUNT DRACULA

In 1897 the Irish writer Bram Stoker published his horror novel *Dracula.* His creation, Count Dracula, remains the most famous of vampires. Every night Count Dracula changed into a bat and flew from his castle to find a new source of blood, which he needed to survive.

### Historical inspiration

The inspiration for Stoker's book was the notorious 15th-century Romanian warrior-prince, Vlad IV. Although an outstanding soldier in his country's defense against the invading Turkish and Hungarian armies, Vlad gained lasting notoriety for his cruelty: Between 1459 and 1461 he was estimated to have tortured and murdered over 100,000 men, women, and children. He was known as *Tepes*, meaning "Impaler," because his favorite method of torture was to impale his victims on spikes. In Romanian the word *dracul* means "devil," and from this Bram Stoker derived the name Dracula.

reopened, the corpse would not have deteriorated as much as expected, since the victim would have died more recently than was thought. The corpse might also have a frightful expression on its face and blood on its hands, since the victim would have suffocated while trying to claw a way out of the coffin.

Some scholars have pointed to a rare blood disease as another possible source of the vampire legend. At the end of the Middle Ages inbreeding among eastern and central European nobility gave rise to a rare genetic disorder called congenital erythropoietic porphyria. Sufferers produce too much porphyrin (a substance basic to the formation of red blood cells) in their bone marrow. Individuals thus affected shun daylight because it causes skin lesions, which crack and bleed. The excess of porphyrin also causes reddening of the skin and the eyes. Doctors of the time treated the condition by encouraging their patients to drink blood. It may be that rumors of these nighttime blood drinkers gave rise to many of the vampire stories that circulated in eastern and central Europe.

The vampire of Slavonic folklore is a creature usually described as a resuscitated corpse, sometimes skeletal, sometimes merely gaunt, but always equipped with full red lips and canine teeth for drawing blood.

***Evil deterrent***
*On the Nicobar Islands in the Bay of Bengal, in the Indian Ocean, painted wooden statues, with vampire-like fangs, are used to ward off evil spirits.*

# A woman by day, the azeman is by night a wild animal that prowls in search of human blood.

This vampire is far removed from the Hollywood version, which is often portrayed as a person who changes into a bat.

It has been suggested that the idea of a bat acting as a vampire was incorporated into the legend when followers of the Spanish explorer Hernán Cortés returned from Mexico in the 16th century. Cortés's soldiers brought back horrifying stories of the vampire bats that they had encountered there.

## Supernatural entity

In many regions of the world there is a vampire equivalent in folklore and myth. The Chinese fear their version, a demon who inhabits a corpse, more than any other supernatural entity. When someone dies, the family keep watch over the body, because it is believed that if a cat jumps over the corpse, the

*Mark of the vampire*
*If you turn this picture of a 1922 German bank note 90 degrees counter-clockwise, you will see a hooded vampire sucking blood from the young man's neck. This image was incorporated in the note as propaganda. It symbolized the new Germany being bled dry because of the reparations demanded by the victorious nations at the Treaty of Versailles following the First World War.*

deceased person will become a vampire. The appearance of the Chinese vampire is more frightening than that of its European counterpart. It has glaring eyes, long claws, and is covered with greenish-white hair. It, too, can fly.

## Peppery protection
In Surinam, South America, the azeman is a lethal combination of the vampire and another man-into-beast transformation, the werewolf. A woman by day, the azeman is by night a wild animal that prowls in search of human blood. Fortunately, there is an antidote to its powers. A broom propped across the doorway will bar it from entering a house. Peppercorns or rice scattered on the ground will force the azeman to count each grain; if the creature is still counting at sunrise, it will be transformed back into its human form and can be captured.

Residents of Trinidad are especially suspicious of any woman who comes to their home asking to borrow either matches or salt. This is because such a woman may be a sukuyan, or vampire, and if they give her what she requests, she will have the power to suck their blood at night as they sleep. Local legend holds that if the occupants of the household place a cross in their window, she will be rendered powerless.

## Vengeful ancestors
According to the Ashanti tribe from Ghana, West Africa, the sasabonsam is a vampire that sucks blood from the thumbs of a sleeping person. In Guinea, West Africa, the owenga are vengeful ancestors, or bad spirits, that return from the dead to feast on human blood.

On the island of Grenada in the West Indies, the loogaroo is the equivalent of the vampire. This creature appears as an old woman and prowls through the night in search of blood, which she has pledged to the devil.

In Mexico the civateteo were evil vampire witches. Believed to be the spirits of women who had died during childbirth, they took revenge on children by spreading among them childhood diseases, such as infantile paralysis.

## LUST FOR BLOOD
Throughout history notorious murderers have displayed a sickening bloodlust. Reports of these depraved monsters' deeds have helped perpetuate the legend of the vampire.

### Drinking human blood
The 15th-century French baron Gilles de Rais, who earlier in his life had fought alongside the French warrior-maiden Joan of Arc, was reportedly possessed of an irresistible urge to drink human blood. He disemboweled over 150 live children for this purpose. Known as the Black Baron, de Rais was burned at the stake.

### Kidnapped maidens
Countess Elisabeth Bathory, a 17th-century Hungarian noblewoman, was reputed to have killed young girls and then drunk, and even bathed in, their blood. Bathory believed that this would preserve her looks. The macabre compulsion apparently began when the countess's maid accidentally pulled her hair while combing it. Her mistress slapped the unfortunate girl and drew blood. It was claimed that tasting the blood that dropped on the countess's hand caused her bloodlust. Eventually brought to trial, the countess ended her days sealed in her own bedchamber.

*Modern vampire?*
*Marcello Costa de Andrade was accused in February 1992 of murdering 14 boys in Rio de Janeiro, Brazil. He claimed to have drunk the blood of some of the boys because he believed it would make him as handsome as his young victims.*

# VAMPIRES AT THE MOVIES

*From the first moment in 1922 when the sinister, fang-toothed, and cadaverous figure of Nosferatu filled the screen, the bloodcurdling legend of Dracula has provided endless inspiration to filmmakers.*

### Dracula (1958)

Audiences were kept on the edge of their seats by the chilling special effects in this British vampire movie. Christopher Lee, who has played the part of Count Dracula more often than any other actor, manages in his portrayal to combine both the horror and the strange seductiveness of the bloodthirsty count. In a still from the film (above) he cowers in terror as he is confronted by a cross. In the poster (below) he violates a victim.

### Dracula (1931)

Hollywood's first attempt at the genre remains perhaps the most famous vampire movie. Bela Lugosi plays Dracula. His pallor and black cloak have become the trademarks of Count Dracula in vampire movies ever since. When it was first released, *Dracula* was billed as "a strange love story." Lugosi subsequently appeared in half a dozen vampire movies during the 1930's and 1940's.

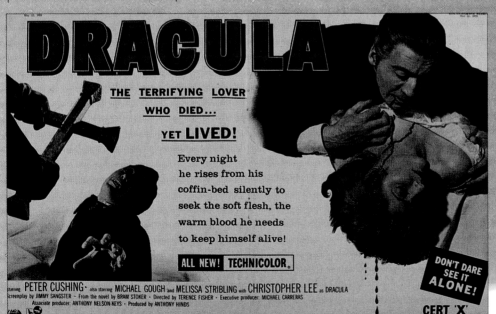

### The Vampire Bat (1933)

A series of atrocious murders baffles the authorities. All the clues point to the deaths as the work of a vampire. Investigations lead to one man: a fanatical scientist named Dr. von Niemann (played by Lionel Atwill). His charming assistant, Ruth (Fay Wray), just happens to be the police investigator's fiancée. Transformed into a bat, von Niemann flies through the night in search of his victims. After putting his fiancée's and his own life in danger, Inspector Karl Brectschneider (Melvyn Douglas) finally outwits and destroys the vampire.

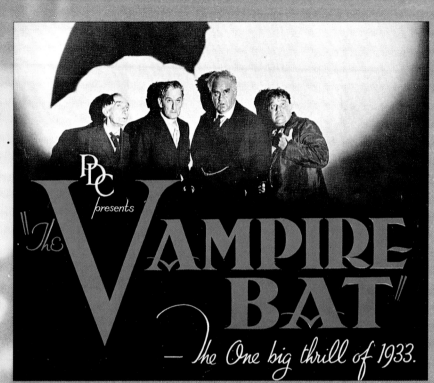

PDC presents "The VAMPIRE BAT"
— The One big thrill of 1933.

### Nosferatu *(1922)*

*The first vampire movie (background picture) is as terrifying today as it was when made in Germany more than 70 years ago. Max Schreck plays the hideous vampire, complete with pointed ears and skull-like face, who lures his victims to his sinister castle in central Europe. Loosely based on Bram Stoker's novel* Dracula, Nosferatu *is very powerful cinema despite being a silent movie.*

### The Lost Boys (1987)

The wilder excesses of delinquent teenagers take on a new meaning in this modern vampire tale. Set in the Californian seaside town of Santa Cruz, the movie depicts a band of rebellious teenagers who roar around the neighborhood on motorbikes at night, and start behaving strangely after drinking from a wine bottle containing human blood. The brother of one of these tearaways notices that his sibling has changed. He sleeps all day, is out all night, wears dark glasses, and casts no reflection in a mirror....

### House of Dark Shadows (1970)

New England is the location for this vampire B-movie. The Collins family welcome into their house a stranger who claims to be a cousin from England. They accept him because he closely resembles a portrait of one of their ancestors. Before long, strange deaths occur. The mysterious cousin is unmasked as a vampire just as he is about to suck blood from the sleeping governess.

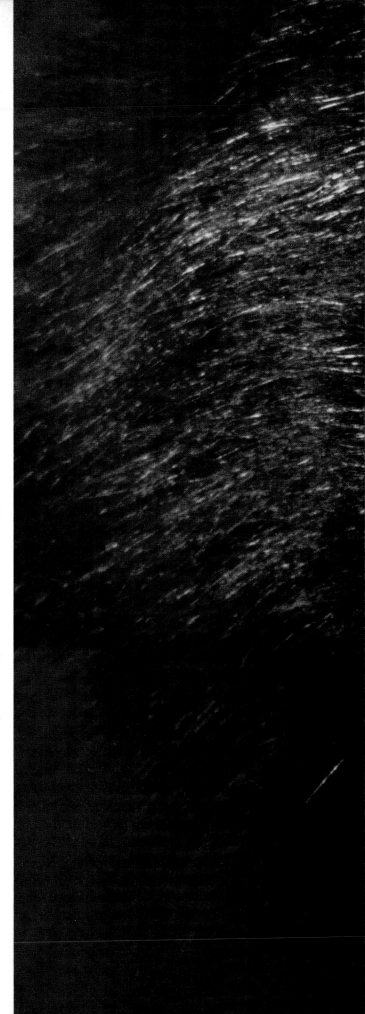

# WEREWOLVES

*Whether they become werewolves in western Europe, were-hyenas in Nigeria, or were-jaguars in South America, human beings who can transform themselves into predatory animals have persisted in legend since ancient times.*

*I*N 1573 IN A VINEYARD near the small town of Dôle in eastern France, a 10-year-old girl was playing. Suddenly a strange four-legged creature reportedly leapt at her, knocked her down, and sank its fearsome teeth into her neck. The wolflike beast then dragged the girl into a nearby wood, where it tore the flesh from her bones with its teeth and claws.

A month later this same creature apparently attacked another young girl in the neighboring village of La Pouppé. Just as it was about to dispatch the terrified girl, three villagers, alerted by her screams, came to the rescue. Witnesses described the creature that scurried away into the woods as bearing an uncanny resemblance to a local hermit. Soon the wolf-man struck once again — this time in the vineyard of Gredisans, near Dôle. After pouncing on and killing a young boy, it made a meal of his flesh.

> ## Suddenly a strange four-legged creature leapt at the girl, knocked her down, and sank its fearsome teeth into her neck.

When the news that the beast had killed again spread throughout the region, enraged villagers organized a massive hunting party. On September 13, 1573, a legal decree was issued that allowed the residents of Dôle to "assemble with javelins, pikes, arquebuses, and clubs to hunt and pursue the werewolf, and to take, bind, and kill it without incurring the usual fine or penalty for indulging in the chase without permission."

### Secret salve

The villagers did not take long to corner their quarry. He turned out, as some had already suspected, to be the local hermit, Gilles Garnier. The villagers were convinced that Garnier was a werewolf — a man who could turn into a wolf, complete with a full coat of fur, pointed teeth, and sharp claws.

At his trial on January 18, 1574, Garnier claimed that while walking in the woods he had met a "phantom in the shape of a man," who showed him how to rub himself with a certain secret salve, which would

## THE BEAST OF GÉVAUDAN

Between June 1764 and June 1767, a series of hideous killings occurred in a mountainous region of southern France called Gévaudan. Some women and children were devoured; others were simply torn apart. The killer soon became known locally as the Beast of Gévaudan.

### Fantastic creature

A peasant woman from the village of Langogne claimed to have seen the beast. She described it as walking on two legs, covered with short red hair, and having a snout like a pig. Panic spread as the locals feared the worst: that the beast was a *loup-garou* (meaning "werewolf"), which could commit its dreadful acts as a wolf and then change itself back into a man to avoid detection.

### Tracking the beast

Local inhabitants petitioned King Louis XV for help. On September 21, 1765, a party of 40 local hunters led by the king's personal gun-carrier, Antoine de Beauterne, found and shot their quarry near the village of Pommiers. The creature proved to be a black wolf, six feet long and weighing 143 pounds.

However, the murders did not stop. Then, in June 1767, a local hunter shot a wolf near Gévaudan with a silver bullet that had been blessed. (This was a traditional means of destroying a werewolf.) Thereafter, the Beast of Gévaudan claimed no more victims.

### Rabid wolves

Many theories have been put forward to explain the killings. One explanation is that a number of wolves had been infected with rabies and this made them attack people. Another theory was that the deaths were the work of one or more human serial killers.

**Ferocious as a beast**
*This sixth-century Swedish die shows a warrior wearing a wolfskin. Scandinavian warriors sometimes had representations of fearsome creatures embossed on their helmets, believing it would make them fiercer in battle.*

**In wolf's clothing**
*American artist George Catlin (1796–1872) devoted his life to studying the American Indians. Here, one of Catlin's paintings shows a medicine man of the Blackfoot tribe wearing a wolfskin, which was believed to imbue its wearer with the animal's fearsome qualities.*

transform him into a werewolf. Once he had anointed himself, his feet and hands were transformed into paws, his body became covered with a pelt of fur, and he was able to run on all fours.

Horrified villagers heard Garnier explain how, after killing his first victim, he found the taste of human flesh so addictive that he carried part of the corpse home and offered to share it with his wife. Garnier was sentenced to death by burning at the stake. The most likely explanation of Garnier's confession is that it was the result of mental illness or was extracted under torture.

## Evil creature

In medieval times a large population of wolves existed in Europe. A fierce beast of prey with glowing eyes and a spine-chilling howl, the wolf was held in the popular imagination to be an evil, even demoniac, creature. It was probably from this concept that the wolf-man legend arose. And the legend undoubtedly provided a popular explanation for the violent excesses of some mentally ill people.

Wolf-men have featured in legends since ancient times. In Greek legend, Lycaon, the king of Arcadia, attempted to win favor with Zeus by sacrificing a child to the god. For this action Zeus transformed Lycaon into a wolf. The Roman writer Pliny the Elder (A.D. 23–79), in his *Persian Wars*, wrote of the Neuri, a Scythian tribe, whose members allegedly became wolves once a year.

In the first century A.D. the Roman satirist Petronius recorded the story of a Greek man who, it was claimed, one night saw a young soldier strip off his clothes and change into a wolf. In this guise

**Leopard imitation**
*In Cameroon, West Africa, women paint their faces with spots in imitation of the leopard, before taking part in a dance to honor the beast.*

he received a laceration in his neck. When he changed back into his human form, the soldier was found to have a wound in exactly the same spot.

Shamans (doctor-priests) and witch doctors believed that by covering their bodies with a wolfskin they might become infused with the strength, agility, and ferocity of this animal. For the same reason, ancient Norse warriors, the Berserkers, who were notorious for the frenzy of their attacks, wore bearskins when they went into battle.

## Indigenous wild animals

Although the legend of the werewolf exists only in Western cultures, other cultures have somewhat similar legends that substitute for the wolf a wild animal native to their country. As Frank Hamel noted in *Human Animals* (1915): "Every part of the world chooses a special animal...and naturally enough the animal is one which is common to the district."

In Argentina, Uruguay, and southern Brazil — regions that are free of wolves — legend holds that men can turn into pigs or dogs. In some areas girls keep away from boys who live near stockyards, because they are rumored to change into wild dogs or pigs, the *lobisón*, on Saturday evenings. Men are also believed

## LYCANTHROPY

The second-century physician Marcellus of Sida was among the first to describe the condition that we recognize in modern times as lycanthropy (from the Greek for "wolf man"), in which the patient thinks he or she has become wolf-like or actually turned into a wolf.

Marcellus noted that sufferers usually had a yellow complexion and hollow eyes, and spent their nights at the tombs of Athens. Other physicians claimed that those afflicted with the disease also suffered from excessive growth of body hair. Lycanthropes were reported to howl wildly and could not be convinced that they were not wolves.

### Melancholy humor

In a 17th-century work, Simon Goulart described victims of lycanthropy as "so dominated by their melancholy humor that they really believe themselves to be transformed into wolves. This malady...is a sort of melancholy, of a black and dismal nature. Those who are attacked by it...imitate wolves in almost every particular, and wander all night long among the cemeteries."

### Modern diagnoses

Today the medical profession believes that the symptoms of lycanthropy are the result of psychological delusions. In more brutal times, the mentally ill were misunderstood, and supposed wolf-men were burned at the stake.

### Frothing at the mouth

In the past, frothing at the mouth was also interpreted as a sign of werewolfism. It is possible that in many cases this was the symptom of canine rabies. This fatal and highly contagious condition would cause an affected animal to attack and bite any living thing within reach, thereby spreading the disease.

This might also explain the belief that a person attacked by a werewolf was also condemned to become one.

**Flesh-devouring beast**
*The horrifying wolf-man depicted in this 16th-century engraving by the German artist Lucas Cranach may actually represent a man who has contracted rabies.*

---

to be able to take on the form of a jaguar, the *tigre capiango*. Legend has it that thieves and soldiers would often adopt this guise. A 19th-century Argentine general, Facundo Quiroga, was said to command a regiment that was composed entirely of were-jaguars. The Navajo Indians of Arizona and New

> ## In the Bornu language of northeastern Nigeria, the word *bultungin* means "I change myself into a hyena."

Mexico believe in individuals that can transform themselves into evil, animal-like creatures and move at enormous speeds. According to legend, the *Yee Naaldlooshii* (meaning "those who trot about with it") dress in wolfskins and resemble werewolves. Several sightings of these "skin walkers" have been reported in recent times, and in one instance witnesses claimed the creatures were running faster than 45 m.p.h. Africa has a wealth of man-animal transformation legends involving were-hyenas, were-lions, and were-leopards. Indeed, in the Bornu language of northeastern Nigeria, the word *bultungin* means "I change myself into a hyena." The famous Scottish explorer David Livingstone noted that the Makololo people believe certain individuals, the *Pondoro*, can turn themselves into animals. Livingstone met a man whom villagers claimed could assume the form of a lion. When the explorer asked for proof, the villagers refused, saying, "If we ask him to do so, he may change while we are asleep and kill us."

### Leopard Men

The Leopard Men of West Africa were a murderous secret society who caused terror well into the 20th century. Dressed in leopard skins, which they believed imbued them with that beast's strength, they attacked their victims using three-pronged knives to simulate the claw marks of the leopard they venerated.

**Werewolf protection**
*According to folklore, wolfsbane will keep a werewolf at bay.*

# HOWLING AT THE SCREEN

*The idea of a man turning into a ravening wolf is so terrifying that horror-movie makers have found this transformation a continuing inspiration. And some of these films have adopted an unmistakably tongue-in-cheek approach to the subject.*

### The Wolf Man (1941)

Universal Studios produced many of the classic horror movies of the 1930's and 1940's, including *Dracula* (1931) and *Frankenstein* (1931). The unfortunate wolf-man in this movie is one Lawrence Talbot, the heir to an English stately home, who has the misfortune to be bitten by a werewolf. Lon Chaney, Jr., plays the wolf-man, who is dispatched at the end of the film.

### Curse of the Werewolf *(1961)*

*This film (background picture) is based loosely on Guy Endore's novel* The Wolfman of Paris. *Leon (played by Oliver Reed) is the illegitimate son of a servant girl and a beggar who has been unjustly imprisoned. At the full moon Leon turns into a werewolf and terrorizes the local community that ostracized his parents.*

He always wanted to be special ...but he never expected this!

TeenWolf

A NEW COMEDY STARRING MICHAEL J. FOX OF "BACK TO THE FUTURE"

AN ENTERTAINMENT RELEASE

### Teen Wolf (1985)

Michael J. Fox is a teenager who discovers that he is the last of a long line of werewolves. When transformed, this teenage werewolf is endowed with extraordinary physical prowess, which makes him the most popular kid on the basketball court. Following on the success of other 1980's horror movies with comic undertones, such as *The Howling* and *An American Werewolf in London*, *Teen Wolf's* treatment of the theme of lycanthropy is played strictly for laughs.

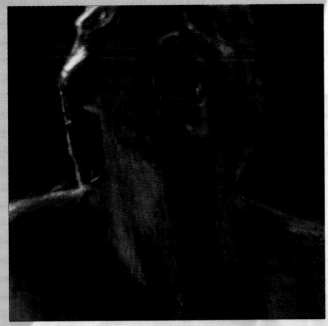

### An American Werewolf in London (1981)

Two young American tourists get lost on the Yorkshire moors in the north of England one night and are attacked by a local werewolf. One dies, but the other survives and becomes a wolf-man who terrorizes London whenever there is a full moon. The transformation scenes are astonishingly convincing, and the sound track features a witty collection of moon-associated songs, such as "Bad Moon Rising" and "Blue Moon."

### The Howling (1980)

A TV anchorwoman badly in need of a vacation goes to stay at a California commune only to discover that its members are werewolves. The film includes many clever references to previous werewolf films, and manages to be funny as well as scary.

### The Company of Wolves (1984)

This adult fairy tale, adapted from a novel by English writer Angela Carter, tells of a time when grandmothers would warn young women to beware of men "whose eyebrows meet in the middle and who are hairy on the inside." The film is set in a dreamworld and features striking and imaginative sets. It explores the psychological origins of lycanthropy, and although the transformation effects are not as elaborate as in other modern werewolf pictures, the film makes a fascinating addition to the genre.

# BENIGN BEASTS

**Although many transformations of humans into beasts inspire fear, some gentler metamorphoses involve change that is thought to benefit humankind.**

ONE SUMMER'S EVENING, according to folklore, a fisherman on one of the Orkney islands, off Scotland, saw a school of seals swimming toward shore. They came up onto the land, and he watched transfixed as the seals shed their skins. Transformed into a handsome band of men and women, they began to dance with a bewitching grace that belied the seals' clumsiness when on land. The fisherman was entranced by the beauty of one of the seal-women in particular. While the creatures were engrossed in their dancing, the fisherman stole the sealskin of the woman who had attracted him.

When the creatures finished their dance, they resumed their familiar seal form and returned to the sea. But the seal-woman who

## A fisherman saw a school of seals swimming toward shore. They came up onto the land, and he watched transfixed as the seals shed their skins.

had lost her skin could not return with her companions. According to the story, the seal-woman now had to live on land until her sealskin could be restored to her. The fisherman and the seal-woman eventually married and had several children. But the seal-woman always longed to return to the sea. In the end one of her children found her sealskin where her husband had hidden it. The seal-woman donned her skin and immediately regained her seal form, whereupon she abandoned the land and returned to the sea. The mythical creatures in this folktale were "selkies," the gentle seal-people who appear in the legends of the Scottish islands.

### Descended from seals

Folktales such as the Shetland ballad "The Great Selchie o' Sule Skerry" tell of romances between the islanders and seal-people. There is still a belief among Scottish islanders that certain physical characteristics indicate descent from such unions: Horny excrescences of skin

**Serpent mother**
*The legends of the Australian Aborigines tell of a mythical creature called the All-Mother. Appearing as Nagloya, the Rainbow Serpent, this creature gave birth to the Aborigine people. Here, the legend is depicted in a modern bark painting by the Aboriginal artist Yirawala.*

on the hands and feet, for example, are interpreted as traces of webbed fingers and toes.

In many tales the selkies help people in distress, such as ship-wrecked sailors. Often the selkies ask those they have saved from drowning to help find the lost sealskin of one of their number. Traces of these beliefs live on in the Shetland and Orkney islands. To this day islanders claim that killing a seal invites misfortune.

### Sealskin kayaks

However captivating these stories may be, some folklorists have offered a more down-to-earth explanation of the origin of selkies. They suggest that they may have been misidentified fishermen from Iceland or Scandinavia, who came to the Orkney and Shetland islands in their sealskin-covered kayaks. As James R. Nicholson notes in *Shetland Folklore* (1981): "With their bodies concealed inside their sealskin vessels and with their short paddles dipping into the water, they would certainly have appeared more like seals swimming than men rowing."

### Half-man, half-snake

In Asia, far from the windswept Orkney Islands, *nagas* (snake gods) are often thought to take on human form. In Buddhist mythology and art they are often represented as half-snake and half-human, a strange commingling of man and animal. As Jean P. Vogel, author of *Indian Serpent Lore*, explains: "In the legends

### Heart's ease

*The Milanau people of Sarawak, northern Borneo, believe* nagas *(snake gods) live at the bottom of rivers and cause heart disease. Local tradition has it that the illness can be transferred onto a carved wooden effigy of a naga, such as the one below, by means of an incantation. The effigy bearing the disease is then cast into the river.*

### Temple guardian

*A female* naga *(snake god) guards the entrance to an 11th-century temple in Bhubaneshwar, India.*

they [nagas] usually exhibit a bewildering blending of human and serpentine properties; they may even act entirely as human creatures, yet there can be no doubt that their real nature and form are those of the serpent."

### Water snakes

The naga can be beneficial to man. Just as selkies frequently come to sailors' assistance in times of distress, so nagas are thought to help communities by providing much-needed water. They are said to haunt lakes, ponds, and sources of rivers, thus controlling the water needed for irrigation and basic survival. To this day, many cisterns and water tanks in India bear a sculpture of a naga.

Sometimes nagas appear to take on an entirely human form, and in this guise marry human wives. Frank Hamel in *Human Animals* (1915) tells the tale of a raja, an Indian prince, who traveled to a distant land, where he fell in love with and married a princess. When the time came to return to his kingdom, his new wife refused to depart until he revealed his true lineage. The raja attempted to persuade his wife that she did not need to know. However, when he saw this was to no avail, he agreed to her request.

### Serpent into stone

The raja then took his wife to a river. He warned her that she must not be alarmed at what she saw. If she showed any fear, he said, she would lose him forever.

**Magical charm**
*Crocodiles are the most formidable carnivores on the island of Madagascar, and they are held in great awe by the natives. This carved wooden war charm was believed to be imbued with magical properties.*

Slowly the raja began to lower himself into the water. As he did this, he asked if his wife still wished to know his true lineage. Soon the raja was submerged up to his neck. He dived under the water and reappeared in the form of a naga. The wife cried out in distress, at which point the raja was turned into a stone.

### Descended from snakes

So strong is the belief in nagas that some Indians even claim to be descended from them and to be able to transform themselves into the legendary man-serpents. It is said that the rajas of the town of Nagpur in central India were descended from a naga.

The belief that some human beings can be transformed into animals is common in Africa. In Zaire, central Africa, it is believed that village sorcerers could change themselves at will into a crocodile.

### Harmless crocodiles

According to Zairian folklore, crocodiles were generally harmless creatures unless they had been possessed by a sorcerer. If anyone was killed by a crocodile, a human was usually blamed. After such an attack, villagers would begin looking for the person suspected of bewitching the animal and causing it to kill.

The Konde tribespeople of Malawi, southeast Africa, had a unique method of dealing with anyone suspected of such a transgression. They would tie up the unfortunate guilty party and lash him to a fish trap, where he would remain until he, too, was taken by a crocodile. On the island of Madagascar, in the Indian Ocean, the Zafandravoay, or "sons of the crocodile," are a clan within the Antandroy people. They believe they are descended from a woman who married a crocodile. They have no fear of the reptiles, believing each is inhabited by the spirit of a dead villager.

### Charity rewarded

Madagascan legends often stress the link between humans and crocodiles. In one legend, a tribe traced its ancestry to one woman who lived in a village on the shore of what was once Lake Anivorano. One day she offered a thirsty stranger a drink, after he had been refused one by all the other villagers. The man turned out to be a sorcerer and warned the woman to move to higher ground. Angered by the other villagers' lack of charity, the sorcerer then flooded the region. All the villagers, except the woman, were drowned and transformed into crocodiles.

### Ceremonial burial

If a Madagascan villager was killed by a crocodile, hunters would trap one of the reptiles and kill it as humanely as possible — with poles instead of spears, apologizing all the while. The crocodile would then be wrapped in elegant cloths and receive a ceremonial burial.

> **Crocodiles were regarded as generally harmless creatures unless they had been possessed by a sorcerer.**

**Toothless crocodile**
*This painted wooden crocodile mask is used in a Mexican folk festival, during which the spirit of the creature is worshiped.*

# CHILDREN OF THE WILD

***Throughout history there have been reports of children who have grown up among wild animals. These children often appear to have taken on the characteristics of their animal foster family.***

**The "gazelle boy"**
*The Bedouin tribespeople who found the gazelle boy had to tie his feet and hands to prevent him from running away.*

O N OCTOBER 17, 1920, a party of men, led by Indian missionary Rev. J. Singh, armed with shovels and bows and arrows, surrounded a wolf's den in dense jungle near Midnapore in eastern India. A week earlier Singh had seen two "monsters" leaving the cave with the wolves. As diggers sank their shovels into the den, two wolves bolted out and vanished into the jungle. A she-wolf remained guarding the entrance. The villagers killed her with arrows.

Deep inside the cave, Singh was startled to find two cubs huddled in a ball together with two human children. Both girls were naked, had thick bushy hair, and crawled on all fours. Both had heavily calloused hands, knees, and elbows. Their tongues hung out and both frequently bared their teeth. News of the Midnapore wolf-children flashed around the world.

Singh brought the two bewildered wolf-children, whom he named Amala and Kamala, to his orphanage in Midnapore. Amala, whom Singh estimated was about 18 months old, died a year later. Kamala, however, who appeared to be about eight years old when found, lived with Singh and his wife for several years, until her death on November 14, 1929.

### Ran on all fours

In a letter published in the *American Journal of Psychology* in 1926, Singh described Kamala as "possessed of very acute hearing and...an exceedingly acute animallike sense of smell. She can smell meat at a great distance...is fond of pouncing upon any killed animal if found anywhere by her...used to cry or howl in a peculiar voice, neither animal nor human." Both girls ran on all fours and ate their food in a crouching position. When approached, the girls used to arch their backs and shake their heads in a menacing posture.

Over the years Kamala learned to walk upright and perform simple actions such as drinking from a glass. By the end of her life she had a vocabulary of about 30 words. Numerous experts examined her

and agreed that she was not mentally retarded. Rather, as French anthropologist Lucien Malson has noted, "her pitiable condition was due only to the lack of a proper family so early in life."

Many well-documented reports of feral, or wild, children have surfaced through the ages. Feral children have been reported to be reared by cattle, monkeys, goats, leopards, antelopes, sheep, and even pigs. In 1990 a boy reported to have been raised by a herd of goats was found in the Andes, in Peru. Apparently he had been abandoned as a toddler and lived with the goats for nearly eight years, eating roots and berries and drinking their milk. Sri Lankan hunters claimed to have spotted a naked teenage girl in 1976 living in the jungle with a herd of buffaloes. Investigators believed that she was an illegitimate child who had been abandoned when young, and then reared by female buffaloes.

> **Feral children have been reported to be reared by cattle, monkeys, goats, leopards, antelopes, sheep, and even pigs.**

### "Gazelle boy"

Feral children usually take on the habits of their animal foster parents. In 1971 French anthropologist Jean-Claude Armen discovered a boy living among a herd of gazelles in North Africa. The "gazelle boy,"

**Wolf-boy**
*An illustration from Rudyard Kipling's classic children's stories,* The Jungle Books *(1894–95), which tell the story of a boy reared by a family of wolves.*

who appeared to be about 10 years old, leapt and jumped about like a gazelle, twitched his ears and scalp at the slightest noise, and sniffed everything around him. The boy had developed thick, strong ankles, and when running he could almost match the incredible bursts of speed of a gazelle.

However, some outlandish and poorly documented reports of feral children can be discarded as obvious fakes. For example, a recent report of an Australian girl supposedly raised by kangaroos was soon shown to be a hoax.

### "Deliberately abandoned"
Experts are divided when it comes to establishing the mentality of feral children. Some, such as the French social anthropologist Claude Lévi-Strauss, believe that the majority "are congenitally abnormal children who have been deliberately abandoned."

Noted child psychologist Bruno Bettelheim believed that many feral children were actually autistic. But others disagree. Jean-Claude Armen observed that an abnormal, or subnormal, child would have little chance of surviving in the wild.

### Natural idiots?
Psychologist Robert Zingg from the University of Denver, who examined the Midnapore children and has conducted many studies on feral children, wrote in the October 1949 issue of The *American Journal of Psychology*: "It would seem improbable that out of some 30 creditable cases of feral man, pure chance should have operated to the result that all should be natural idiots."

Feral children have existed. But the way in which they came to live among their animal guardians more often than not remains a tantalizing mystery.

*Noble savage?*
*As a child, Victor Pinel survived for many years in the wild.*

### THE WILD BOY OF AVEYRON
On August 1, 1799, a party of men were hunting in the woods of Caune in Aveyron, in central France. Suddenly they were astonished to see a naked boy guarding a hoard of roots and acorns. Startled by the hunters, the boy swiftly climbed a tree. The men gave chase and captured him.

### Back to civilization
So it was that the Wild Boy of Aveyron, as he was called, was brought back to civilization. Local officials named him Victor Pinel. It appeared that as a child, Victor had become lost when wandering through the woods. He had probably survived by living on nuts and roots.

At first, officials were convinced that Victor was a hopeless idiot, until he was put in the care of Jean-Marc Itard, a teacher at a school for deaf mutes in Paris. After five years of intensive study with Itard, Victor was able to stand, speak a little, wear clothes, and perform some simple tasks, such as using a fork and spoon.

Itard kept meticulous records of the progress of his work with Victor. This research has become a textbook for the education of the mentally subnormal.

### L'Enfant Sauvage (The Wild Child)
*Victor was the subject of a film made in 1970 by the French film director François Truffaut.*

# TALES OF TRANSFORMATION

*Legends, myths, and fairy tales from around the world have often told of magical transformations of man into beast. In many cases, the metamorphosis is the result of some evil enchantment, which can sometimes be undone by the good deeds of others.*

*Illustration by Warwick Goble from* **The Fairy Book** *(1913)*

### Beauty and the Beast

In a classic French fairy tale, a merchant steals a rose from a deserted castle garden. Suddenly the Beast who rules this castle appears. For his theft, the merchant must forfeit his life or send to the castle one of his daughters in his stead. The merchant's youngest daughter, Beauty, goes to the castle and in time she comes to respect her captor. One day she returns late from a visit to her sick father and finds the Beast dying. Beauty declares her love for the Beast. At this he is transformed into a handsome prince. Beauty's love has broken an evil enchantment.

### The Frog Prince

In one of the fairy tales collected by the Brothers Grimm, a princess drops a golden ball down a well. A frog appears and says he will retrieve it if she promises to eat and sleep with him. The princess agrees, and so the frog retrieves the ball. That evening the frog arrives at the castle. The irritated princess lets him eat with her. But when they retire to bed, she flings the frog against a wall, at which he is turned into a prince.

*Illustration by Walter Crane from* **The Frog Prince** *(c. 1874)*

### Jealous goddess

In Greek legend, Zeus, the king of the gods, fell in love with the nymph Io. When his wife, Hera, suspected the affair, Zeus turned Io into a beautiful white heifer to protect his lover from the jealous Hera. But Hera demanded that Zeus give her this very heifer as a gift. She had the heifer guarded by Argus, a creature with a hundred eyes, to prevent Zeus from transforming Io back into a nymph. Io's father and sisters begged that Io be restored to them. Finally Hera relented, and Io regained her human form.

*Illustration of the story of Io from a 16th-century French manuscript*

## The Minotaur

In Greek legend, Pasiphaë, the wife of King Minos of Crete, gave birth to a creature with a man's body and a bull's head, which was named the Minotaur. Minos built a labyrinth in which to hide the monster. No one who entered the labyrinth ever escaped from the Minotaur. Then the warrior Theseus came to Crete. With the help of Ariadne, Minos's daughter, he entered the maze and slew the monster.

ORIGINE DELLARTE MAG
CHI COMINCIO DACHI E S
RESTO DELLE MEDICINE

ABBIAM
giche negl
gione o illu
te con breu
ſa degna d
che ſia fra
no ha haui
do & in tu
hauere acq
che eſſa ſo

*Illustration from a 15th-century Venetian manuscript, showing a magician summoning up a satyr and minotaur*

## Circe

In Greek legend, Circe was a sorceress notorious for changing men into swine. On the journey home after the Trojan War, the Greek leader Odysseus and his companions sailed to the island of Aeaea, where the witch lived. Before long Circe had bewitched Odysseus's companions and turned them into pigs. However, the god Hermes had given Odysseus the herb moly, to protect him against Circe's magic. Safe from her spells, Odysseus compelled Circe to restore his companions to their human shape.

*"Circe" (1891), painting by J. W. Waterhouse*

*Illustration by John D. Batten from* **The Children of Lir** *(1892)*

## The Children of Lir

In Celtic legend, when King Lir's wife died, her sister, Olfa, came to comfort the king. Olfa grew jealous of the king's love for his four children and turned them into swans for 900 years. When this time had passed, the Children of Lir regained their human form, but no sooner were they changed than their bodies withered and they immediately died.

# CHAPTER FIVE

# BEASTS OF MYTH AND LEGEND

*Mermaids, unicorns, centaurs, dragons, basilisks, griffins, manticores — over the centuries man's fertile imagination has conjured up a fascinating assortment of fabulous beasts, some benevolent, some malign.*

"From the navel upward, her back and breasts were like a woman's...her body as big as one of us; her skin very white; and long hair hanging down behind, of color black; in her going down they saw her tail, which was like the tail of a porpoise, and speckled like a mackerel."

This remarkable account of the sighting of a mermaid is taken from the journal of

## FAKES AND RELICS

In 1842 the showman P. T. Barnum exhibited in New York what he claimed was a preserved mermaid. Crowds flocked to see what Barnum himself described in his autobiography as "an ugly, dried up, black-looking, and diminutive specimen." "The Fejee Mermaid," as Barnum called it, was undoubtedly one of many 19th-century fakes, which were usually created by stitching the upper half of a small, shaved monkey to the lower half of a fish.

## "Unicorn's" remains

But not all alleged remains of mythical animals are hoaxes. Some have been misidentified. In 1700 the remains of a "unicorn" were discovered in a clay pit on the bank of the Neckar River in Switzerland. Duke Eberhard Ludwig took possession of them and donated a portion to the city of Zürich. But paleontologists eventually established that the bones were the remains of lions and other animals. What had been originally identified as the "horn" of a unicorn turned out to be a mammoth's tusk.

the English navigator Henry Hudson. He was describing what two of his crew, Thomas Hilles and Robert Raynar, claimed to have seen on June 15, 1608, when looking overboard from Hudson's ship off the coast of Novaya Zemlya, a group of islands off northern Russia.

## Fatal song

In Hudson's account there is no suggestion of the alleged mermaid behaving like a siren, but it is as a siren that the mermaid has long been portrayed. Bewitchingly beautiful, sometimes sitting on a rock and combing out her long tresses with the aid of a hand-held mirror, at other times swimming gracefully offshore, and singing an irresistibly seductive song, she entices sailors to their doom — either luring their craft to destruction on a reef or dragging the mariners down to a watery grave. In this, the mermaid is a romantic personification of the allure and danger of the sea.

## Half-fish gods

The origins of a half-human, half-fish creature date back to earliest history. The Babylonian god of the waters, Oannes, was portrayed on relief carvings either as a fish-headed, fish-skin-caped man or as a true merman — that is, a man with a fish's tail. The first recorded mermaid goddess was a moon deity known to the Syrians as Atargatis. This goddess was believed to have been originally entirely human in form, but, it was said, she was filled with shame after bearing a daughter by a handsome young man and cast herself into a lake, whereupon her lower half turned into a fish's tail.

In Greek mythology, Triton, son of Poseidon, god of the sea, was a merman who gave his name to a number of minor sea deities, who were collectively called tritons. In his *Description of Greece* the Greek traveler and geographer

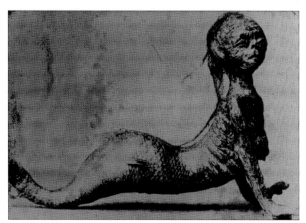

**Hoax catch**
*In the 19th century many fake mermaids were produced by joining together parts of different creatures. This specimen was alleged to have been caught alive in 1874 at Bristol, England.*

**Sea sport**
*"Nereid and Triton" by Peter Paul Rubens (1577–1640) depicts a triton (merman) sporting with a nereid (sea nymph). In Greek mythology both were attendants of Poseidon, the sea god.*

Pausanias (*fl.* A.D. 143–176) made the startling claim to have seen two tritons: "Their bodies are bristling with very fine scales....They have gills behind the ears and a human nose, but a very big mouth and the teeth of a wild beast....From the breast and belly down they have a dolphin's tail instead of feet."

Triton was not the only member of the Greek pantheon with a fish's tail. Artemis, the virgin huntress, was also sometimes

> **Bewitchingly beautiful, the mermaid is a romantic personification of the allure and danger of the sea.**

depicted in this way, although she was reputed to be a creature not of the sea but of fresh water.

The siren of Greek myth, whose song was supposed to lure mariners to their death and who is now identified with the mermaid, was originally not a half-fish creature at all but a woman with the body of a bird. It was not until about 300 B.C. that the siren exchanged her feathers for a fish's tail, and it is as a mermaid that she has been depicted ever since.

◆ PAGE 104

A pair of manatees in the Crystal River, Florida

# THE MERMAID MYSTERY

*Encounters with mermaids are generally attributed to missightings of various sea mammals. But the speculations of one eminent marine biologist raise an intriguing question: Could there exist in the sea humanoid creatures as yet unknown to science?*

MANY RESEARCHERS probing the world of myth and legend believe that the creatures certain observers have identified as mermaids have in fact been sea mammals of one kind or another. For example, the mermaids that Columbus thought he saw are believed by scientists to have been manatees, one of the two families of sea cows. These large, slow-moving mammals, which inhabit the Caribbean and the coastal waters of West Africa, often appear in an upright position above the water (they need to surface in order to breathe), suckling their young. The theory suggests that sailors who had been at sea a long time and starved of the company of women, may, on viewing this humanlike picture of maternity, have thought the manatee to be a kind of demi-woman.

## Ugly and ungainly

Other reports of mermaids have been attributed to sightings of dugongs, the other family of sea cows (found in the Indian Ocean and western Pacific). They are smaller than manatees but have similar habits. In 1982 anthropologist Dr. Roy Wagner, of the University of Virginia, reported seeing mermaid-like creatures off the island of New Ireland, Papua New Guinea. But closer investigation revealed these mysterious beasts to be dugongs.

The problem with linking all "mermaids" with sea cows is that the former are usually described as beautiful and graceful, while the latter are ugly and ungainly. In *Zoo Quest to Guiana* (1956) celebrated British wildlife author and TV presenter Sir David Attenborough describes a manatee as follows: "She was not a pretty sight. Her head was little more than a blunt stump, garnished with an extensive but spare moustache on her huge blubbery upper-lip. Her minute eyes were buried deep in the flesh of her cheek...."

## "Beautiful, limpid eyes"

A more convincing marine candidate for the mermaid is probably the seal. In *Sea Fables Explained* (1884) Henry Lee writes: "The round, plump, expressive face of a seal, the beautiful, limpid eyes, the hand-like fore-paws, the sleek body, tapering towards the flattened hinder fins...might well give the idea of an animal having the anterior part of its body human and the posterior half piscine." In addition, the seal habitually basks on rocks, as mermaids are said to do, and, whereas sea cows have no voice, some listeners claim that the seal utters melodious sounds.

But could mermaid sightings be based on a creature as yet unknown to science? In 1960 eminent British marine biologist Sir Alister Hardy speculated that man's apelike ancestors might have passed some evolutionary time in the sea.

If such sea apes did exist, is it possible that some might have remained in the sea instead of moving onto land? Such an idea is purely speculative, but, as Irish author and researcher Peter Costello wrote in *The Magic Zoo* (1979): "We could imagine that some of these apes...might give rise to stories of mermaids. By now, after several million years...aquatic man...would be a very strange creature indeed."

## CREATING A UNICORN

Over the years various travelers reported having seen unicorns. But in 1827 the French zoologist Georges Cuvier claimed that the unicorn was a physical impossibility. If the unicorn was a cloven-hoofed animal, he said, the front of its skull must, like that of all other such animals, also be cloven. But, if this was the case, a horn could not grow from the center of its forehead.

### Massive horn

In 1934, however, American biologist Dr. F. W. Dove proved Cuvier wrong. Dove took a day-old bull calf, trimmed each of its two horn buds, and transplanted them to the center of the animal's forehead. As the bull grew, it developed a massive single horn. Although the horn allowed it to dominate the rest of the herd, it had a gentle nature. Dove had created a type of unicorn, raising speculation that this fabled creature might once have existed as a freak of nature.

*Horn transplant*
*At Marine World in Ukiah, California, several goats have been transformed into "unicorns" by transplanting two horn buds to the center of the forehead.*

### "She never spake"

Images of mermaids, and myths about them, abound in the art and literature of the world (there are carvings of them in many medieval cathedrals) — but of particular interest are the various encounters with these creatures that have been reported throughout history.

In 1403, for example, at Edam, in Holland, some women and their servants claimed to have found a mermaid stranded in floodwater from the sea. Describing this event in his *Speculum Mundi* (1635), English minister John Swan wrote: "She suffered herself to be clothed and fed...she learned to spin and perform other petty offices of women...she would kneel down with her [mistress] before the crucifix, she never spake, but lived dumb and continued alive (as some say) fifteen years."

### Columbus's sighting

On January 4, 1493, Christopher Columbus, nearing the end of his first voyage of discovery in the Americas, entered in his journal that, off the coast of Haiti, he and his crew had seen three mermaids rise high from the sea: "They were not as beautiful as they are painted, although to some extent they have a human appearance in the face...." Columbus also noted that he had seen similar creatures on an earlier voyage, off the coast of Guinea, West Africa.

Among the considerable catalog of more modern alleged sightings, one of the most remarkable is that which took place in about 1830 on the island of Benbecula off northwest Scotland. The account claimed that a woman washing her feet in the sea saw a mermaid, that the creature escaped (but not before being hit in the back by a stone), and that a few days later its dead body was washed up on the shore.

The British folklorist Alexander Carmichael heard this story, he reported, from

> "The hair was long, dark and glossy....The lower part of the body was like a salmon."

"persons still living who saw and touched this curious creature." In *Carmina Gadelica* (1900) he wrote: "The upper part of the creature was about the size of a well-fed child of three or four...with an abnormally developed breast. The hair was long, dark and glossy, while the skin was white, soft, and tender. The lower part of the body was like a salmon, but without scales."

The sheriff of the island was said to have had a coffin made for the mermaid, which was buried on the shore.

### Purity and virility

Just as romantic a creature of myth as the mermaid is the unicorn, a pure white, cloven-hoofed, horselike beast with a single, spiraled, white horn in its forehead. Regarded as a symbol of both purity (its color) and virility (its horn), the unicorn was portrayed in medieval bestiaries (collections of moral tales about animals) as a swift, fierce, solitary animal that could be captured only in a certain way. In *A Dictionary of Fabulous Beasts* (1971) British writers Richard Barber and Anne Riches describe the method: "A virgin, preferably both beautiful and naked, [was] bound to a tree; at which the unicorn, attracted by a creature as rare and chaste as itself, would approach, and meekly lay its head in her lap; and this would so entrance it that it could easily be killed by the hunter waiting in ambush."

### Religious allegory

This myth became transformed into a religious allegory, that of the Holy Hunt, which was depicted in countless medieval paintings, sculptures, and tapestries. In this, it can be said, the maiden represented the Virgin Mary, the unicorn Christ, the animal's horn the unity of Father and Son, and its death the Crucifixion. A beautiful version of this allegory — one in which the maiden is clothed — is depicted in the Unicorn Tapestries, a masterpiece of French Renaissance art, in the Metropolitan Museum of Art in New York City.

The first known references to the unicorn are in the Gilgamesh verse epic of ancient Mesopotamia, dating from about 2000 B.C., and in the Hindu epic poem the "Mahabharata" (*c.* A.D. 400). But from classical times onward, belief in the existence of the unicorn flowed from two sources. One of these sources was a history of India by the Greek historian and physician Ctesias (*fl.* 400 B.C.). Ctesias wrote: "There are in India certain wild asses which are as large as horses....Their bodies are white, their heads dark red, and their eyes dark blue. They have a horn on the forehead which is about a foot and a half long....The animal is exceedingly swift and powerful, so that no creature...can ever overtake it."

Zoologists believe this extraordinary, colorful creature to have been a mixture of the Indian rhinoceros, the onager (the Asian wild ass), and a considerable amount of wild imagination.

The other source for belief in the unicorn was the Bible. The Authorized Version has nine references to the

Hebrew scholars in the 3rd century B.C. when they translated the Bible into Greek. They rendered the Hebrew *re'em* (meaning "aurochs," a wild, long-horned ox by then extinct in the Holy Land) as *monoceros* (meaning "single-horned"), which in translations from the Greek became "unicorn." As a result the Scriptures seemed to lend weight to the belief that the animal existed.

## The lion and the unicorn

The unicorn's traditional enemy was the lion, which in medieval fable was said to defeat its foe in the following way. The lion would run to a tree, inviting the unicorn to charge it. As the unicorn drew near, the lion would move aside, and the unicorn, driving its horn into the tree, would become wedged fast. The lion would then fall upon its helpless foe.

In the British royal coat-of-arms, however, the two animals represent not conflict but union. They came together in 1603, when James VI of Scotland, upon becoming James I of England, added the Scottish unicorn to the English heraldic lion.

### Poison test

During the Middle Ages and the Renaissance, what were claimed to be unicorn horns were sold throughout Europe for great prices. They were used to make eating and drinking vessels. It was believed that if these sweated, the food or drink in them was poisoned. Elizabeth I kept such a horn at Windsor, and there was another at the French court (now in the Musée Cluny, Paris).

In 1638, however, the Danish zoologist Ole Wurm proved that these "unicorn" horns were in fact the tusks of narwhals, small whales found in Arctic waters.

***Sacred beast***
*A man dressed to represent a unicorn takes part in a traditional ceremony of the Kwakiutl Indians of the American Northwest Pacific Coast. The unicorn is one of their sacred animals.*

***Unicorn allegory***
*This 16th-century French tapestry in the Musée Cluny, Paris, is one of a series of allegories of the five senses, all featuring a maiden and a unicorn. This one is entitled "Sight."*

animal, among them: "God brought them out of Egypt; he hath as it were the strength of an unicorn." (Numbers 23: 22). Yet the biblical references appear to be due to a linguistic error made by

# FABULOUS HORSES

*The horse is one of the creatures that appear most often in myth and legend, where it is usually invested with supernatural powers, most commonly the ability to fly.*

**Heavenly journey**
In "Apollo," a painting by the Italian Renaissance artist Pietro Perugino (*c.* 1450–1523), four horses draw the golden chariot of the Greek sun god on its daily journey across the sky.

**Magical mount**
A flying horse is one of several supernatural creatures that appear in the Eastern collection of folk tales *The Thousand and One Nights.* In this illustration by Edmund Dulac, Sinbad rides such a horse high above a city.

**Way to go**
An illustration by Andrew Lang in a 1905 edition of *The Arabian Nights Entertainments* shows another enchanted, though wingless, horse. It transports the prince and princess of the tale to the capital of Persia.

*Footsore centaur*

## Half-man, half-horse
The centaurs of Greek mythology were a race of creatures with the head and torso of a man and the lower half of a horse. They were portrayed as riotous, brutish, and lecherous, and personified man's baser instincts. "Centaur in the Village Blacksmith's Shop" (above) is a modern treatment of the centaur myth by the 19th-century Swiss artist Arnold Böcklin. "Pallas and the Centaur" (below), by the Italian Renaissance painter Sandro Botticelli (1445–1510), illustrates no known Greek myth and is probably an allegory depicting chastity overcoming lust.

*Soothing the beast*

### Winged steed
Pegasus, the winged horse of Greek myth, is shown here in a mural by the French artist and author Jean Cocteau (1889–1963), which is in the town hall in Menton, France. Pegasus was said to have sprung from the blood of the snake-haired female monster Medusa, after Perseus had killed her.

# THE GOOD, THE BAD, AND THE UGLY

*In the East the dragon is perceived as predominantly gentle and good-natured, but in the West it has always been portrayed as ferocious and malign. Could it be that the dragon of Western myth is based on memories, locked within the collective unconscious, of grotesque and fearsome beasts, survivors from the age of dinosaurs?*

IN WESTERN CULTURES THE DRAGON has always been the most malevolent and terrifying of all mythical beasts, the embodiment of evil. The powerful legend of St. George or St. Michael slaying the dragon — the subject of so many medieval and Renaissance works of art — is in fact an allegory of the triumph of Christianity over evil.

In the West the dragon traditionally has the head and body of a serpent, lizard, or crocodile; giant, bat-like wings; the legs and clawed feet of a lion or eagle; and a barbed tail. Its great fanged mouth breathes scorching fire. In legend, it usually terrorizes an entire community, sometimes demanding the sacrifice of a young virgin, until eventually a heroic young man triumphs over the monster — usually by impaling or beheading it — and rescues the maiden.

## Sacrificial offering

The familiar European legend of the dragon first appeared in *The Golden Legend*, a 13th-century compilation by the Italian scholar Jacob of Voraigne. The story recounts that in Silene, Libya, St. George rescued a princess who had been offered as a sacrifice to a

**Rescuing a maiden**
*St. George kills a crocodile-like dragon and rescues its intended victim, in this painting by the 19th-century British artist Sir Edward Burne-Jones.*

pond creature with poisonous breath. This story may be based partly on the Greek myth of Perseus rescuing the beautiful, enchained Andromeda from a sea monster. But there may also be a factual basis for the tale. The Welsh writer Gwyn Williams has linked the Silene of legend with El Aggar u-Silina, a stretch of water in present-day Libya. And he has suggested that the pond

## In legend, the dragon terrorizes an entire community, sometimes demanding the sacrifice of a young virgin.

monster may have been a crocodile sacred to a local tribe, which ritually sacrificed virgins to the animal until a Christian knight suppressed the practice.

The word dragon derives from the ancient Greek *drakón*, meaning "serpent" — and in classical times a dragon was simply a huge snake. Nearly 2,000 years ago, in *Historia naturalis*, the Roman scholar Pliny the Elder described the Indian dragon as a serpent "so enormous as easily to envelop the elephant with its folds and encircle it with its coils." (He was probably describing an Indian python, and he was either exaggerating or portraying one far more powerful than any known specimen.) In the Bible the term dragon is used in the same way: "And the great dragon was thrown down, that ancient serpent, who is called the Devil and Satan...." (Revelation 12: 9).

### Merciless enemy

To the Christian world, then, the dragon has most often represented the forces of darkness. In the eighth-century Old English epic poem *Beowulf*, for example, the dragon is described as the merciless enemy of mankind, as in this passage (from a translation into modern English by the American poet Burton Raffel):

> *Vomiting fire and smoke, the dragon*
> *Burned down their homes....*
> *And the signs*
> *Of its anger flickered and glowed*
> *in the darkness,*
> *Visible for miles, tokens of its hate*
> *And its cruelty....*

In the East, however, the dragon has generally been seen as mild and gentle. Together with the tortoise and two mythical creatures, the phoenix and the kylin, the dragon is one of the four sacred animals of China,

***Death of a dragon***
*In this illustration to the 11th-century Persian epic poem "Shah-nameh" ("Book of Kings"), the hero Rustam kills a dragon, in the second of his seven trials.*

***Real-life monster***
*Some cryptozoologists have suggested that the dragon may have been based on sightings of the Komodo dragon, a fierce, carnivorous, grotesque-looking lizard native to Indonesia.*

where it is known as the *lung*. It is usually portrayed as a large crested reptile, with a bearded head and open jaws, and wingless — though still capable of flight. It is associated with water and is believed to have the power to unleash rain during a drought.

The dragon was also used as the Chinese imperial symbol, and throughout the Far East today images of it are a feature of many ceremonies and festivities. Yet to the Chinese, too, the dragon can be destructive as well as benign: they believe that, if angered, it can send storms and floods.

### Giant lizards
In the 19th century, fossil evidence of the existence of the pterodactyl, an extinct winged reptile, led to the speculation that dragons, far from being purely mythical, may at one time have been

> Dragons, far from being purely mythical, may at one time have been real monsters that had survived from the age of the dinosaurs.

real monsters that had survived from the age of the dinosaurs. In *Mythical Monsters* (1886) New Zealand geologist Charles Gould declared: "We may infer that it [the dragon] was a long terrestrial lizard, hibernating and carnivorous...possibly furnished with wing-like expansions...."

### The Komodo dragon
A discovery that took place in 1912 gave some support to Gould's theory. A Dutch pilot who crash-landed on the island of Komodo in Indonesia reported seeing huge, grotesque-looking, carnivorous creatures resembling dragons. Investigations confirmed the airman's story. The animal he had seen was a giant monitor lizard, now known as the Komodo dragon. The creature grows to 10 feet in length, has a long, powerful tail, feeds on carrion, and sometimes attacks and kills people. From New Guinea, too, have come unconfirmed reports of lizards that are even larger than the Komodo dragon.

It is, however, difficult to understand how these particular giant lizards, isolated in a part of the world remote from Europe, could have played any part in the development of the Western legend of the dragon.

Could it be that the Western dragon developed from a memory in the collective unconscious of modern man, a memory of other, widespread, fierce and fearsome animals, survivors from the age of dinosaurs — a memory passed down from our primitive ancestors, who lived in terror of such creatures?

# LETHAL GAZE

*A mythical creature somewhat like a miniature dragon, the basilisk, it was believed, could kill with either its baleful eyes or its venomous breath.*

"WOULD THEY WERE basilisks to strike you dead!" cried Lady Anne in Shakespeare's *Richard III*. She was speaking of her eyes, whose beauty the evil Richard had just praised. The fearsome basilisk was thought to be able to kill with a glance. Just as deadly as the creature's gaze was its foul breath, which allegedly killed plants, animals, and people. There were only two recommended methods of killing the creature. One was to hold a mirror up to it, so that it would slay itself with its own look. Even as late as the 16th century, this technique was reportedly used in Warsaw to kill a so-called basilisk. The other method was to set a weasel on the creature.

***Weasel power***
*The only creature thought capable of withstanding a basilisk's deadly stare and destroying the monster was a weasel, as shown in this illustration from a medieval bestiary (collection of animal fables).*

## Small snake

In appearance and reputation, the basilisk underwent a transformation over the centuries. It originated — as so many creatures of myth did — in the pages of Pliny the Elder's *Historia naturalis*. Pliny describes a small, brightly spotted snake, which he termed *basileus* (meaning "little king"), perhaps because the spot on its head resembled a crown.

By the late Middle Ages, however, the basilisk, though retaining its serpent's body, had acquired the head and legs of a cock and the alternative name of cockatrice. The reason was that in the 12th century the British naturalist Alexander Neckham originated a myth that the basilisk was born from an egg laid by a cock in a dunghill and hatched by a toad.

The idea of a cock's egg — which was reputed to have a skin instead of a shell and to be spherical rather than ovoid — was probably based on the appearance of the egg-like tumor that is sometimes found in the bodies of old male domestic fowl.

> In the Middle Ages a myth was originated that the basilisk was born from an egg laid by a cock in a dunghill and hatched by a toad.

It seems unlikely that there could be any basis in reality for such a weird creature as the basilisk. Yet, as documented by British zoologist Dr. Karl P. N. Shuker in his *Extraordinary Animals Worldwide* (1991), an animal remarkably similar has been reported living in central Africa and the Caribbean. Known as the crowing crested cobra, it is — according to those who claim to have seen it — an extremely large, venomous male serpent with a cock's-comb-like crest, facial wattles, and a cockerel's crow.

Over the years various reports have been published about this animal. In 1944, for example, a Malawi physician, Dr. J. O. Shircore, announced in the journal *African Affairs* that he possessed parts of one of these creatures — a portion of the neck and the skeleton of the comb.

It is possible that it was ancient travelers' tales of the crowing crested cobra that originally gave rise to the myth of the cockatrice — but it is unlikely that we shall ever discover whether this theory is true or not.

# DRAGONS OF THE WORLD

*Of all mythical beasts, the dragon is the most universal, appearing in the literature and art of many cultures. Presented here are some of the striking images of it that have been fashioned around the world.*

**Benevolent beast**
This painting of a Chinese dragon is on a dish dating from the reign of the emperor Yung-cheng (1723–35). Despite the typically bearded, scowling head of this example, the Chinese dragon was seen as a predominantly benevolent creature.

**Servant of the god**
In this 16th-century French illustration to a book of astronomical poems, a double-headed dragon draws the chariot of the Greek god Cronus.

**Serpent's body**
Chinese dragons usually have the body of a scaly serpent, as seen in this gilt-bronze sea dragon of the Six Dynasties period (A.D. 295–589).

*Chinese dragon design of the 14th century*

*Chinese dragon design
of the 14th century*

**Seven-headed Satan**
This 14th-century German
altarpiece illustrates an
allegorical biblical passage
(Revelation 12: 1–5), in which
the seven-headed, ten-horned
dragon represents Satan, and
the child symbolizes Christ.

**Fiery breath**
The ability to breathe fire, as displayed by this
dragon from an English bestiary of about 1300,
may have been based on the venom-spitting
behavior of certain cobras.

**Expansive by nature**
The extensive, uncoiling body
of this dragon decorates a villa
door in Singapore. In the East
it was believed that dragons
could expand to fill all heaven
and earth.

# WINGED WONDERS

*From the Egyptian phoenix, celebrated symbol of rebirth, to the Sri Lankan devil-bird, with its bloodcurdling screams, some mythical birds, generally thought to be purely imaginary, may in fact once have been real.*

T THE TOP OF A PALM TREE a bird's nest catches fire. It has been ignited by a spark struck from the hooves of celestial steeds drawing the chariot of Ra, the Egyptian sun god. Amid the flames a beautiful Arabian bird extends its golden neck and purple wings, but instead of flying off, it dances. Eventually, it is consumed by the fire and reduced to ashes....

## The phoenix reborn

But this is not the end. Indeed, it is only the beginning — for 500 years later a new bird is reborn from the ashes. It seals the remains of the nest in myrrh, wraps it in aromatic leaves, and molds it into the shape of an egg. This it carries as a sacred offering to the temple of the sun at Heliopolis, then flies away to paradise. Five hundred years later it returns to earth, where it begins again the cycle of self-immolation and resurrection — a process that continues forever.

## A beautiful Arabian bird is consumed by fire....500 years later a new bird is reborn from the ashes.

This bird, the phoenix, originating in the mythology of ancient Egypt, has become a universal symbol of rebirth and the most famous of all fabulous birds.

## Enemy of snakes

One of the earliest, yet mightiest, of fabulous birds was the Indian garuda. Originally, it was reputed to be an enormous bird of prey with a golden body and scarlet wings, which carried the great Hindu god Vishnu through the sky. Eventually, however, the garuda acquired human arms, legs, and torso. It was thought to be an indefatigable enemy of all snakes, including those that Buddhists considered divine. As a result, they regarded the garuda as a demon.

More noble, more beneficent, was the Persian simurgh. Initially a griffin-like (lion-bodied) bird, with a formidable beak containing sharp teeth, the simurgh later assumed the shape of a true bird, one with glorious plumage and immense wings. Its touch was believed, in Persian folklore, to heal instantly even the most terrible of wounds.

The original home of the simurgh was supposedly the fabled Tree of Knowledge, whose branches were festooned with the seeds of every plant that has ever existed. When the simurgh took flight, it was said, its powerful ascent shook the tree's branches so violently that the seeds were scattered throughout the world, bringing a wealth of valuable plants to mankind. Later, according to myth, the simurgh nested in seclusion on the sacred Persian mountain of Alburz, far beyond the climbing abilities of any man.

### Sinbad's ride

So colossal that its wings could eclipse the sun, so strong that it could carry off elephants, the roc was the mythical Arabian bird on whose foot Sinbad, in the Eastern collection of tales *The Thousand and One Nights*, was carried off to a mountain. Although this fabulous creature was described as eagle-like, the actual bird on which it was probably based was flightless — the ostrichlike giant elephant bird *Aepyornis maximus*, which is believed to have inhabited Madagascar until about 1700.

Like the roc, whose egg Sinbad mistook for the cupola of a great building, the

***Splendid simurgh***
*The simurgh, a noble, gloriously plumed bird of Persian myth, is seen here surrounded by other, smaller birds in a 15th-century illustration to the "Conference of the Birds," by the Persian poet 'Attar (c.1142—c.1220).*

giant elephant bird laid enormous eggs (with an internal volume of about two gallons). Many semi-fossilized specimens have been discovered.

### Man-eaters

No less formidable were the Stymphalian birds of Greek mythology — crane-sized, ibis-like, man-eating creatures with brass beaks, wings, and claws, said to have colonized the Stymphalian marsh in Greece. The sixth of the 12 great labors assigned to the mythological hero Heracles (Hercules in Roman myth) was to drive these birds away. Athene, goddess of wisdom, gave him a pair of brass castanets. They made such an appalling noise that the terrified birds rose in flight, and Heracles then brought many of them down with arrows.

The Stymphalian birds have always been considered to be purely imaginary. But in 1987 Swiss ornithologist Michael Desfayes suggested that they may

***Garuda and god***
*An 18th-century Nepalese gilt-bronze carving of a garuda depicts this half-human bird of Indian myth trampling upon its sworn enemy, a snake god.*

actually have been based upon a real (and harmless) bird, the bald ibis, now restricted in Europe to a single locality in Turkey.

Another mythical bird that may owe something to an actual species is the halcyon. This bird with brilliant blue plumage was said to build a floating nest on the Aegean a week before the winter solstice (December 22). To enable it to do so, it was believed, the gods pacified the wind and waves — and this was also beneficial to sailors. (From this myth came the expresssion "halcyon days" — a time of peace and contentment.) The belief that the halcyon may have been based on the kingfisher, a land bird with iridescent blue plumage, is reflected in the fact that many kingfishers have the zoological generic name *Halcyon*.

## Ambivalent nature

In some parts of the world there is still widespread belief in the existence of fabulous birds. In Japan, for example, many people still fear the tengu, a sinister, aggressive, birdlike creature equipped with wings, talons, and a long beak. It is said to hatch from a gigantic egg. Few people will travel through forests or mountains where tengus are claimed to live. But occasionally, so it is said, such creatures will defy their reputation and help people in trouble.

A bird that occupies the shadowy borderland between myth and reality is the Sri Lankan devil-bird. According to a popular myth of that country, retold in Sir J. Emerson Tennent's *Sketches of the Natural History of Ceylon* (1861), a jealous husband, doubting the paternity

**Enormous meal**
*The roc, a gigantic Arabian bird of myth, seen here in an illustration by E. J. Detmold, was said to feed its young on elephants.*

of his son, killed the child and made a curry of the flesh, which his unsuspecting wife began to eat. Finding her son's finger in the dish, the horrified woman fled to the forest, where she killed herself. According to Buddhist belief, she was then changed into an ulama, or devil-bird, which utters spine-chilling screams of grief.

Such a creature would appear to be pure myth, yet there is said to be an actual bird in Sri Lanka that emits hideous screams. In Tennent's book, a Mr. Mitford, who was reputedly an expert on the island's bird life, gave a graphic description of the bird's cry as "indescribable, the most appalling that can be imagined, and scarcely to be heard without shuddering; I can only compare it to a boy in torture, whose screams are being stopped by being strangled."

### Rarely seen

Although many people have heard the devil-bird's bloodcurdling shrieks, very few have apparently seen the creature, and its true identity remains a mystery. Some ornithologists have suggested that the bird is simply the brown wood owl, but witnesses who claim to have seen the devil-bird say that it has a long tail and cuckoo-shaped body and resembles a nightjar, not an owl. Yet there is no known species of nightjar that screams. So the question remains. Is the devil-bird a figment of the imagination or an actual creature?

> In Japan many people still fear the tengu, a sinister, aggressive, birdlike creature said to hatch from a gigantic egg.

### THE REAL PHOENIX?

In their attempts to identify the gorgeously plumed phoenix of Egyptian myth with a real bird, scientists tended to discount New Guinea's birds of paradise — otherwise likely candidates — because of the island's great distance from Egypt. In 1957, however, Australian zoologists discovered that New Guinea tribes had exported bird of paradise plumed skins for centuries and that among those visiting the island, as long ago as 1000 B.C., had been traders from Phoenicia in the Middle East.

### Sealed in myrrh

Another significant discovery was that the tribespeople used to preserve the skins for export by sealing them in myrrh, molding them into an egg shape, and wrapping this in burned banana skins — a procedure that tallies almost exactly with the mythical bird's reputed treatment of its destroyed nest. Perhaps most significant of all is the fact that the brilliantly colored males of Count Raggi's bird of paradise are adorned with cascades of scarlet feathers that, during their courtship dance, they repeatedly raise aloft, while quivering intensely — a spectacle reminiscent of the phoenix dancing in its burning nest.

On reaching the Middle East, descriptions of this spectacle, combined with the egg-like parcels of skins, may well have been sufficient to inspire the myth of the phoenix.

*The forces of darkness that have always haunted man have assumed in his imagination a variety of powerful, if sometimes bizarre, forms, as these illustrations show.*

## THE MANTICORE

*I*N 1964 A FEMALE FRIEND of the English novelist David Garnett told him a strange story. In 1950 she spent a night at an inn near Granada with a Spanish male companion, who was dark and bearded. The innkeeper complained to her that the servants, who were simple mountain people, were all leaving that day, because of the bearded guest. "They say he is a Mantiquera," the innkeeper told her, "and will steal their babies at night and cut them up and eat them."

### Six rows of teeth

The monster that the Spaniards feared, the manticore (or manticora), first appeared in print in the fourth century B.C. In a work that has not survived, the Greek physician Ctesias claimed that, while at the Persian court, he had seen a bizarre creature, brought there by Indians. It had a man's face, with three rows of teeth in each jaw, a lion's body, and a long tail with a sting like a scorpion's. It was said to abound in India, where it ate men and beasts. Eventually, the manticore found its way into medieval carvings and bestiaries and the works of the earliest naturalists.

The second-century Greek traveler Pausanias suggested that Ctesias' manticore was in fact a tiger. The 19th-century Irish geologist Valentine Ball lent some support to this theory when he pointed out that the manticore's "triple rows of teeth" may have originated in the tiger's distinctive three-lobed molars, and that its "sting" may have been based on "a little horny-dermal structure like a claw or nail" at the tip of the tiger's tail.

*Manticore, carving on the facade of Metz cathedral in France*

*Manticore, illustration from Edward Topsell's **Historie of Foure-Footed Beastes** (1607)*

# THE GRIFFIN

*A* COMPOSITE CREATURE, the griffin (or gryphon) had the head, wings, and forelegs of an eagle, and the body and hind legs of a lion — though there have been variations on these features in different cultures. In European bestiaries the griffin is usually portrayed as awesomely fierce.

The griffin first appeared in carvings in the ancient Middle East and Greece. Then gradually its image became widespread in European art. Though it was often pictured, it was rarely described. One of the earliest written references to it was in "Arimaspea," a long travel poem written in the seventh century B.C. by the Greek mystic Aristeas of Proconnesus. Peoples now thought to be the Chinese and Mongols told him about fierce, gold-guarding monsters that Aristeas called griffins.

## "Hounds of Zeus"

Over the centuries the griffin was allotted a variety of roles. In *Prometheus Bound*, the Greek dramatist Aeschylus (525–456 B.C.) called griffins "the silent hounds of Zeus." And in the 14th century, inspired by medieval comparisons of Christ with an eagle and a lion, the Italian poet Dante made the griffin a symbol of Christ. For others, however, the griffin was a demon that carried off sinners.

If the griffin was based on any actual animal, the most likely candidate is the lammergeier, one of the largest birds in the world, which inhabits mountainous regions of Europe, Asia, and Africa. Its name is a German word meaning "lamb vulture." The creature is alleged, probably mistakenly, to swoop down on lambs and carry them off.

*Assyrian griffin, lithograph of a bas-relief, probably seventh century B.C., on a temple at Nineveh, Iraq*

*Persian gold griffin bracelet, c. 500–400 B.C., part of the Oxus Treasure, British Museum*

*Etruscan griffins, earthenware jug, c. 650–550 B.C.*

*Heraldic griffin, Kew Gardens, London*

"The Destruction of Leviathan," biblical illustration by Gustave Doré (1832–83)

*The arrow cannot make him flee; for him slingstones are turned to stubble. Upon earth there is not his like....he is king over all the sons of pride.*

**Job 41: 28, 33–34.**

# LEVIATHAN

HE ABOVE DESCRIPTION OF LEVIATHAN as one of the forces of evil occurs in one of five biblical passages that mention the monster. To the Hebrew authors of the Bible the term Leviathan was probably only a general one, meaning any great land or sea monster. Their highly colored descriptions of this great beast may well have been based on a variety of creatures they knew or had heard about: the sperm whale, which the Phoenicians hunted; the Egyptian crocodile, whose range at that time extended to Palestine; the African python, rumors of which had reached the biblical lands through paintings of the serpent in Egyptian temples; and the primeval dragon of Middle Eastern myth.

Sperm whale (possibly the original biblical Leviathan): illustration from a 13th-century English bestiary

*Leviathan as a coiled serpent: "The Spiritual Form of Nelson Guiding Leviathan," by the English poet and artist William Blake (1757–1827)*

## Sea monster

However, in a detailed study of sea-monster reports, *In the Wake of the Sea-Serpents* (1968), the eminent French cryptozoologist Dr. Bernard Heuvelmans advanced another theory. He claimed that certain phrases in the description of Leviathan in Job 41 — "When he raises himself up the mighty are afraid" and "His back is made of rows of shields, shut up closely as with a seal" — suggest that the monster may have been a long-necked sea serpent, of which there are many sightings reported today off New England and California.

# BEHEMOTH

*I*N THE POPULAR IMAGINATION the word Behemoth has come to mean any large creature, and, indeed, the Hebrew word *behemoth* simply means "beasts." But both Henri Boguet (1550–1619), the French demonologist, and Madame Helena Blavatsky, the 19th-century Russian mystic, saw Behemoth as a demon — a symbol, like Leviathan, of darkness and evil.

## Hippopotamus-like

The biblical description of Behemoth's habits and strength has led most zoologists to conclude that the creature is probably based on the hippopotamus (though a few opt for the elephant or crocodile). The only line in Job that does not fit this identification is: "He makes his tail stiff like a cedar." English poet, visionary, and artist William Blake portrayed Behemoth (with the water monster Leviathan) in *Illustrations of the Book of Job* (1825). He depicts the beast as a hippopotamus, with tusks, human ears, and a lion's tail.

*The biblical demon Behemoth, 19th-century illustration*

*"Behemoth and Leviathan," 19th-century painting by William Blake*

*Behold, Behemoth...*
*he eats grass like an ox. Behold, his*
*strength in his loins, and his power in the*
*muscles of his belly....Under the lotus*
*plants he lies, in the covert of the*
*reeds and in the marsh.*

**Job 40: 15–16, 21.**

*Behemoth, miniature from a 12th-century English manuscript*

# CHAPTER SIX

# ANIMAL WORSHIP

*The relationship between man and beast is at its most intense when an animal is regarded as sacred — often as an incarnation or symbol of a god. Such sacred animals range from the awesome to the humble, from the man-eating tiger to the dung beetle.*

Inside the temple the light is dim, the air is heady with incense. Before the altar stand ceremonial urns, into which branches have been inserted. Draped over these, intertwining, hardly moving, are countless serpents. From time to time they feed on eggs brought to them in baskets. They are all Wagler's pit vipers, among the most venomous snakes known to man, and in this Buddhist shrine — the Snake Temple of Penang, Malaysia — their devotees

# The snakes are crowned with flowers, showered with rice, and displayed in brightly decorated carts.... They make no attempt to bite their captors.

worship them. Serpents have enjoyed divine status in many different cultures. In the Egyptian pantheon of beasts, for example, the cobra was especially revered — as both a fertility symbol and an incarnation of Wadjet, the national goddess of Lower Egypt. The elaborate golden headdress of the pharaohs often incorporated an image of a cobra representing Wadjet, rearing up directly above the pharaoh's forehead, with hood expanded. It was believed that this lifelike effigy could spit a kind of fatal immaterial venom at anyone seeking to harm its royal wearer.

It was always thought that the cobra on the headdress was modeled on the true Egyptian cobra. But the ringhals cobra — another Egyptian species, noted for the fearsome accuracy with which it spits blinding venom into the eyes — may have inspired the belief in the special deadly power of the effigy.

### Fertility symbol
The cobra has been worshiped throughout Asia, most commonly the spectacled cobra, which has black-and-white spectacle-like markings on the back of its hood. (According to a Buddhist story, these are prints left by the Buddha's fingers when he touched the cobra Muchilinda in gratitude because the snake had shaded him from the sun with its hood while he slept.) Hindus regard the snake as a fertility symbol, and in India a Hindu woman wishing for a child may place offerings of honey or

*Sacred asp*
*The headdress of Ramses II of Egypt, shown here on a giant statue of the ruler at Luxor, includes a carving of the sacred asp, a symbol of sovereignty.*

*Sacred snake*
*The deadly spectacled cobra is worshiped in India. Here it is shown at a snake festival that takes place every August in the town of Bishnupur, Bengal.*

milk outside the holes of spectacled cobras, in the hope of soliciting their favor and thus conceiving. The woman may even encourage the cobras to inhabit part of her garden, where she will regularly feed and worship them.

Ancient Indian snake gods (*nagas*) were sometimes depicted as multi-headed or multihooded cobras, and many temples to these still stand.

### Crowned with flowers
Probably the most striking example of modern Indian cobra worship is the *Naga Panchami* (meaning "Snake Festival"), which takes place each year on July 20 at Shirala, a village in the state of Maharashtra. This festival celebrates the spectacled cobra as the incarnation of Siva, the Hindu god of destruction and regeneration. Worshipers capture cobras in the countryside the previous day and bear them aloft in a joyful procession through the village streets.

The snakes are crowned with flowers, showered with rice, and displayed in brightly decorated carts. Then they are set free inside a temple, before finally being recaptured and released into the countryside the following day.

### Fangs not removed
Astonishingly, these potentially lethal creatures tolerate all this handling, making no attempt to bite their captors. Some zoologists who have attended the festival have suspected that the cobras' fangs or poison glands, or both, have

# THE GOOD SNAKE

## "Our cobra reared itself majestically before the women with hood spread and tongue flickering. It made no attempt to strike...."

SOME YEARS AGO HARRY MILLER, an animal photographer and writer living in the village of Tirumullaivayal in southern India, witnessed an astonishing spectacle. This is his own description of his experience, as reported in the September 1970 issue of the magazine *National Geographic*.

"I noticed that a termite mound on a roadside near my home had been crowned with a garland of marigolds. The people told me that a cobra had been seen entering it...and that this endowed the mound with special religious significance.

**Tiny temple**

"Soon the Tamil women raised a mud wall around the mound, and little groups of them attended there with flowers, burning camphor, and other appurtenances of Hindu ritual. A month later a priest appeared; gifts of money were offered, and through six or seven years a tiny temple grew up around the mound....Termite mounds are often revered in this way, but I was never able to confirm that any really harbored a cobra. I wanted to see and photograph what would happen if a cobra appeared on a termite mound, and I decided to experiment.

"I chose a mound close to my home, making sure that all the village women knew what I was up to. Then one afternoon...I released my largest cobra on the mound in front of the women....They had arrived accompanied by a few men and many children, and were fully equipped with the paraphernalia of worship. We encouraged them to begin, and what happened then astounded us.

"The natural reaction of any cobra surrounded by a noisy crowd is to slide off into the undergrowth. Instead, our cobra reared itself majestically before the women with hood spread and tongue flickering. It made no attempt either to move away or to strike the worshipers.

"Ramu, my assistant, plucked my sleeve. 'Sir, look at old Mootama, our sweeper woman. She's really worshiping it!' And sure enough this good old lady, who has been with us for many years, was worshiping that lordly snake, her eyes rolling, her body swaying from side to side. Presently the other women began to be affected in the same way, and for a whole hour, until we tired of our picture taking, the big snake sat solemnly there within inches of them, for all the world as though it was receiving its natural and sacred due.

"When we asked Mootama for an explanation she said: 'But what did you expect?...To us Nulla Pambu ["Good Snake"] is a manifestation of Lord Siva. The god himself was there, and naturally we worshiped without fear.'"

been removed or rendered harmless. But on examining the snakes, they have found no evidence of surgery. By consciously refraining from inflicting lethal bites on their worshipers, these snakes seem to justify the name by which they are known in Madras: *Nulla Pambu* (meaning "Good Snake").

## Death-defying dance

Even more astounding than the cobra-handling of Naga Panchami are the ritual dances that the priestesses of Burmese snake cults perform with a king cobra. This is the world's largest venomous snake, reaching lengths of up to 18 feet, with a head the size of a man's fist. It is extremely aggressive and can rear up to a height of four feet, giving it a prodigious striking range.

The dance begins when an untamed, untethered king cobra emerges from a cave or receptacle. Dressed in a loose robe, the snake priestess — watched from a safe distance by other members of the cult — approaches slowly and bows to the cobra. She then begins to dance in front of it. In response, the cobra lunges forward, striking at her knees — but at that precise moment the priestess steps slightly to one side, so that the snake bites only her robe. This happens several times. Then suddenly, just as the cobra is fully erect and poised to lunge yet again, the priestess leans forward and

*Half-turtle*
*This image of Kurma, the half-human, half-turtle incarnation of the Hindu deity Krishna, decorates a temple facade in Singapore.*

*Python mask*
*In Benin, West Africa, the python has long been worshiped as the incarnation of the god Danh-gbi. This ritual mask incorporates a stylized carving of the snake.*

kisses it — sometimes on its head, sometimes directly on its mouth. After drawing away instantly, to avoid the strike that inevitably follows, the priestess repeats her kiss, and then does so once more, before finally moving away from the cobra and rejoining her people.

Venomous snakes that have been worshiped in other parts of the world include the horned viper (in ancient Babylon), the adder (in Lombardy, France, and by Celtic druids), and the rattlesnake (by several American Indian tribes).

## Voodoo

But not all serpent worship involves venomous snakes. In Dahomey (now known as Benin), West Africa, the god Danh-gbi is represented in the form of a python. During the time of slavery, Dahomey natives who were transported to Haiti and other parts of the West Indies took this cult with them. In their new land they worshiped the boa constrictor, the New World counterpart of the python. The slaves termed these sacred snakes *voodoo*. This eventually became the name of the traditional religion of Haiti, which combined Roman Catholic ritual with magical elements from Dahomey. The Aztecs of pre-Hispanic Mexico also worshiped the boa constrictor. Their priests reinforced their authority by appearing dramatically wreathed in the coils of huge living boas.

Snakes are not the only cold-blooded creatures to inspire religious awe in man. In Thailand some temples have pools

> Just as the cobra is fully erect and poised to lunge yet again, the priestess leans forward and kisses it.

▶ PAGE 128

# Consecrated Crocodiles

**Ornamented with gold, hand-fed, embalmed after their death, crocodiles were at times as greatly revered as they were feared.**

I N ANCIENT EGYPT, within the city of Shedet, was a lake constantly occupied by a crocodile that the Egyptians designated as sacred. They believed that the creature contained the soul of Sebek, crocodile-headed god of lakes and rivers. When the holy crocodile died, another was chosen to replace it. The Egyptians adorned each with golden rings in its ears and golden bangles on its feet, and priests fed it by hand. Other crocodiles in a nearby pool were revered as the sacred one's family.

When it died, each crocodile was embalmed and placed in an underground tomb. Entire cemeteries containing thousands of these mummified reptiles have been found at Tebtunis and at Maabdeh. Those at Tebtunis were preserved in old papyruses, those at Maabdeh in bitumen-soaked linen. They were of all sizes, ranging from enormous full-grown specimens to newly born animals. Some crocodile eggs were also found in the tombs.

## Christianity beats the crocodiles

It is known that the Egyptians continued to worship crocodiles until as late as A.D. 335, but eventually the introduction of Christianity brought the cult to an end.

Hindus have dedicated the mugger, a broad-snouted freshwater crocodile, to their great god Vishnu. At Karachi, in Pakistan, a great pond is home to many of these reptiles. Known as the mugger pit, it was described in the 1860's by Andrew Leith Adams, who wrote: "[It] contains many little grassy islands, on which the majority of the crocodiles was then basking....The largest crocodile lives in a long, narrow tank separated from the others. The Fakirs and natives who worship in the neighbouring temples, have painted his forehead red — they venerate the old monster.... Strangers are expected to stand treat....Accordingly we had a goat slaughtered...."

In another part of the world, the Olmecs of Mexico developed a religion centering on the crocodile. They revered the reptile as a symbol of agricultural fertility, and in their religious imagery they depicted it with a tail sprouting into vegetation. To the Aztecs, too, the crocodile, which they called Cipactli, was sacred; they believed that, in return for sacrifices, Cipactli would provide corn crops. In their calendar the Aztecs made the crocodile one of the day signs.

The crocodile has been worshiped in Nigeria, Liberia, Ghana, Madagascar, and other parts of Africa; and crocodile symbolism features extensively in the ancient lore of north Australian Aborigines and various tribes in Papua New Guinea.

**Conciliation ceremony**
*In the village of Yenchen, Papua New Guinea, the people perform a ceremony to appease the spirit of the crocodile.*

**Revered reptile**
*This crocodile mummy, in the Louvre museum in Paris, is one of thousands unearthed from ancient Egyptian cemeteries that were reserved especially for them.*

containing what are known as yellow-headed temple turtles. Revered by the Thais for centuries, these small turtles remained unknown in the West until the German zoologist Dr. F. Siebenrock encountered them in 1903. The Thais also worship another species, called the Siamese temple turtle.

One species of turtle probably owes its very survival to its sacred status. In Bangladesh the black softshell turtle was a useful addition to the diet, and was hunted to extinction, except at the shrine of Sultan Bagu Bastan, near Chittagong, where it is still venerated. The turtles have lived in a pond there since 1875, and they are so tame that they can be fed by hand.

### Frog veneration

Although frogs may seem unlikely objects for veneration, they have been worshiped in various cultures. In ancient Egypt, because large numbers appeared each year with the rise of the Nile, they were revered as the incarnation of Heket, the goddess of rebirth. And frogs appear in Greco-Roman art as symbols of resurrection and fertility.

In both the Old and the New World, frog worship has been used to initiate or halt rainfall. (The Bushmen of southern Africa pray to the chameleon for the same reason.) In Colombia the Quinbaya Indians venerated frogs and all other freshwater creatures. And images of frogs played a part in the religion of ancient Peru: Relatives of the deceased would place statuettes of frogs inside their tombs to remind their souls of the world they had left behind.

In parts of Malaysia, Dennys's flying frog is venerated in a unique and

*Shark god*
*The shape of a shark, a creature worshiped by the Solomon Islanders, is incorporated in the head of this wood carving of a sea spirit.*

*Scorpion coffin*
*A carving of the Egyptian scorpion goddess Selket crowns the lid of a small bronze scorpion coffin.*

elaborate way. With membranes between its toes that act like a parachute, this frog can glide through the air for a considerable distance. On certain holy days Malaysians capture one of the frogs, then carry it on its own sacred chair in a parade. The frog is deftly and harmlessly tied to the chair with garlands of flowers, to prevent it from becoming airborne before the parade ends.

### Shark-kissing

No form of animal worship seems more perilous than kissing a king cobra, but until this century the inhabitants of the Polynesian islands of the Central Pacific used to perform a ritual just as dangerous. Stimulated by the narcotic kava, obtained from a pepper-related shrub, *Piper methysticum*, the natives would attempt to kiss sharks in the waters around the islands. They believed that when they were successful, the sharks would be immobilized and rendered permanently harmless.

Several other cultures that have lived in close proximity to them have looked upon sharks as deities. The Solomon Islanders, for example, sacrificed humans to shark gods. They would place their unfortunate victims on stone altars in man-made, water-filled caverns inhabited by hungry sharks.

The Japanese revered the shark as a storm god. And the Vietnamese built shrines to worship the whale shark.

### Sacred scorpions

Yet another cold-blooded creature that has been regarded as sacred is the scorpion. In ancient Egypt scorpions were believed to be the incarnation of the goddess Selket, protector of the intestines of dead people during embalming ceremonies. Selket was depicted either as a goddess wearing a scorpion on her head or as a scorpion with a human head.

# FLAWED DEITIES

*In various parts of the world certain physically abnormal animals, such as albino snakes and four-tusked elephants, have been venerated because of their rarity.*

ALBINO ANIMALS, those lacking normal pigment, and thus color, have fascinated humanity since earliest times, and such creatures, with their white skin and hair and their pink eyes, have often been worshiped. American Indians believed that white buffaloes were the hallowed property of the sun. These animals were extremely rare (only one buffalo in roughly 5 million was an albino), and many Indian tribes, including the Blackfeet, Southern Cheyennes, Mandans, and Omahas, placed immense value on their hides, using them only for their most important ceremonies and sacrificial rites.

In 1867 the trader George Bent came across a fascinating Cheyenne ceremony involving a white buffalo hide. His account was published in *The Cheyenne Indians* (1923) by George Bird Grinnell. The hide was brought on horseback to the camp, where a master of ceremonies painted it blue. Women and children then tied calico, beads, and other gifts to a sacrificial pole, as offerings to the sun. Finally, the master of ceremonies reverently tied the hide to the pole and said fervent prayers.

### Ivory scales, ruby eyes
In India, the most sacred of all cobras are albinos, with their ivory scales and gleaming ruby-like eyes. The ancient Egyptians may also have revered such snakes; archeologists excavating a courtyard inside the temple at Luxor in 1989 unearthed a magnificent 42-inch-tall statue of a white cobra, carved from cream-colored granite. This may have been an image of the snake deity Mertsager, goddess of silence.

In Europe, white snakes have always been associated with magic and the supernatural. Witches were thought to capture white adders to increase their powers.

> ## American Indians believed that white buffaloes were the hallowed property of the sun.

Certain physical deformities in animals have raised them to supernatural status. In the Ituri Forest of Zaire, the pygmies of the region worship any bull elephant born with an extra pair of tusks. The pygmies regard such animals as elephant kings, whose divine powers render them immune to injury by spears.

Sometimes, after a lizard sheds its tail to free itself from a predator, the replacement tail it grows is forked. In the Middle Ages freak lizards of this kind were associated with the devil. Two-headed snakes are still held in awe in parts of rural France.

### Abnormal feet
Excavations of the temples of Tiahuanaco, the great pre-Hispanic empire that stretched from Bolivia to southern Peru, have revealed the skeletons of llamas with abnormal feet — five toes per foot instead of the normal two. Thus it seems that the same physical abnormalities that would cause us to call certain animals freaks of nature served, in many primitive cultures, to elevate them to some form of divine status.

*Idolized oddity*
*In India an albino monocled cobra is held in greater awe than a normal specimen.*

# GODS WITH WINGS

*Perhaps because their natural habitat is the sky, birds have been among the most commonly worshiped of creatures. In their assigned role as gods, many species have been regarded as benign, while others have inspired awe and fear.*

WHEN, IN 1519, the Spanish conquistadores encountered the Aztec king Montezuma at Tenochtitlán in Mexico, they were fascinated by the exquisite, two-foot-long, green feathers in the ceremonial headdresses worn at the king's court. The Spaniards learned that these plumes came from male birds of a species that the Aztecs regarded as sacred, a bird that, in flight, resembled a spectacular feathered serpent, shimmering green above and scarlet below. This bird was the quetzal. Worshiped as the earthly representation of Quetzalcoatl, god of the air, it was venerated by the Mayas as well, and by the inhabitants of Teotihuacán, the great pre-Hispanic Mexican city.

### Plucked plumes
In contrast to the generally accepted custom of obtaining bird plumage through slaughter, the Aztecs

## In flight, the sacred quetzal resembled a spectacular feathered serpent, shimmering green above and scarlet below.

decided to acquire theirs in a more civilized way — they captured live birds, plucked the plumes from them, then released them back into the wild.

In 1825, following the winning of its independence from Mexico, Guatemala commemorated its peoples' long-standing worship of the quetzal by adopting it as a national symbol. The bird's name has been given to the city of Quezaltenango and also to the country's basic unit of currency, the quetzal.

### Incarnation of wisdom
Perhaps the best-known feathered deity of the past is the ibis, which is related to the stork. The ancient Egyptians worshiped this bird as the incarnation of Thoth, god of wisdom, and depicted it on many monuments. Regarded as a harbinger of spring and therefore as a fertility symbol, the ibis was also venerated as a slayer of the winged serpents that were said to invade Egypt from Arabia each year. Like the cat, another of Egypt's sacred animals, the ibis was

*Peacock on high*
*Buddhists worship a mythical golden peacock. Here, at the Burmese festival of Paung Daw U, a fisherman on Lake Inle pays homage to an elevated image of the bird.*

***Sacred quetzal***
*The brilliantly colored quetzal
was held sacred by the Mayas and
Aztecs as the incarnation of
Quetzalcoatl, god of the air.*

***Symbol in stone***
*A carving of a quetzal decorates
a wall in the ruined ancient
Mexican city of Teotihuacán.*

**Soul bearer**

*A wall painting in an Egyptian tomb at Deir el Medina depicts a bennu, a type of heron. The bird was thought to bear the souls of the dead to the next world.*

mummified after death and buried in one of several sanctified cemeteries. The most important of these was near the great temple at Hermopolis, center of the ibis cult. In Africa today the ibis still flourishes south of the Sahara, but in Egypt, where it was once so venerated, it is now extinct.

Another sacred bird of ancient Egypt was the giant, heron-like bennu. Images of this bird commonly appeared in the Books of the Dead — hieroglyphic texts placed in the coffins of the deceased at Heliopolis during the Fifth Dynasty (*c.* 2494–*c.* 2345 B.C.) — because the bennu was believed to bear to the supreme Egyptian god Ra the souls of those accepted for entry into the next world.

### Giant heron?

Unrecognized by experts on the basis of its ancient images, the bennu, like the phoenix, was long assumed to be mythical. Then in 1979 archeologist Dr. Ella Hoch, of the Geological Museum at Copenhagen University, announced that bones unearthed since 1958 at sites in Oman and Kuwait included some of a hitherto unknown species of heron, one probably taller than even the largest known species, the goliath heron.

The bones of this vanished giant were dated to *c.* 2700–*c.* 1800 B.C. Hence, Dr. Hoch considered it likely that this was the bennu in the ancient hieroglyphics and named it *Ardea bennuides* (meaning "bennu-like heron").

A similar kind of discovery was made in Melanesia. Many centuries ago inhabitants of the tiny Isle of Pines, just south of New Caledonia in the South Pacific, worshiped a bird they called the du. Later generations, claiming that the

> # The Mayas called the harpy eagle the moan, and worshiped it as the bird-god of warriors.

**Indian headdress**

*The Tsimshian Indians of the northern Pacific Coast worshiped various birds of prey and wore stylized images of them as headdresses.*

bird had become extinct, passed down oral descriptions of its behavior and appearance. Allegedly, the du was an aggressive, man-sized, flightless bird that was greatly feared. The islanders also claimed that it was never seen to hatch its eggs in the normal way — that is, by sitting on them.

Without tangible evidence to examine, zoologists tended to dismiss the du as just another piece of fanciful tribal folklore. But in 1974, on the Isle of Pines, French anthropologist Père M. J. Dubois excavated the bones of a previously unknown emu-sized flightless bird. Dating of these bones suggested that the bird may have been alive as recently as A.D. 300 — long after the Melanesians had settled the island.

Prof. François Poplin, of the Natural History Museum in Paris, who named the bird *Sylviornis neocaledoniae*, discovered that it had been an immense species of megapode, a chicken-like bird that does not build a nest and sit on its eggs but hatches them by burying them in pits or mounds of vegetation. There is now widespread scientific agreement that the du, far from being a mythical bird, was in fact *Sylviornis neocaledoniae*.

### Bird-god of warriors

Birds of prey have long been venerated by man. In Mexico the Mayas revered the harpy eagle (which they called the moan) as the bird-god of warriors, and in Sierra Nevada the Mono Indians worshiped the black hawk (which they believed to be an eagle) and wore its splendid decorative plumes on their heads. To the ancient Egyptians, the falcon represented Horus, the sky god.

# BEETLEMANIA

**Ancient peoples revered insects as well as birds. The Egyptians worshiped the dung beetle with great fervor, and other flying insects have also been venerated.**

**Symbol of immortality**
*The scarab, a dung-rolling beetle regarded by the Egyptians as a symbol of eternal life, is shown here in a coffin painting from a tomb at Karnak.*

OF ALL SACRED INSECTS, the most famous is the scarab, or dung beetle, which was worshiped in Egypt. This winged insect makes a ball of dung, rolls it along the ground into a hole, and lays eggs inside it. When the larvae hatch, they feed on the dung and eventually leave it as young beetles. This apparent emergence of new life from waste matter, a process that baffled the Egyptians, caused them to hail the scarab as a symbol of eternal life. Because of the ray-like projections on the beetle's head, they also looked on it as an incarnation of Khepri, the sun god; the dung ball represented the revolving earth.

> ## The Egyptians hailed the scarab as a symbol of eternal life.

## Immortal souls

In honor of the scarab's sacred status, the Egyptians fashioned precious stones — including emerald, jade, and malachite — in the beetle's likeness. Inscribed with hieroglyphs, these carved gems, also known as scarabs, were then placed in tombs or beneath the wrappings of mummies, to grant immortality to the souls of the dead. Eventually, scarab stones lost their religious significance and were worn simply as lucky charms.

## Butterfly dance

Because of its fragile appearance, its often beautiful wings, and its fluttering movements, the butterfly has been identified with the human soul in many cultures. The Hopi Indians of New Mexico and Arizona perform a ceremonial butterfly dance, called the bulitikibi, each year. The young people perform the dance in the village square, in the belief that this celebration will produce a good harvest.

In the Solomon Islands the natives believe that when a person dies his or her soul leaves the body and flies heavenward in the form of a butterfly.

Since they carry diseases and inflict bites or stings, flies are generally regarded as pests. Nevertheless, they have been venerated in some cultures. The Canaanites of ancient Palestine and Syria, for example, sometimes represented their god Baal by idols carved in the shape of flies. And, as the Roman scholar Pliny the Elder (A.D. 23–79) noted in *Historia naturalis*, Greek priests at a religious festival attempted to rid the participants of the unwelcome attentions of flies by invoking the insects' deity, a fly god.

## Sacred stag beetle

Norsemen regarded the stag beetle as sacred to the thunder god Thor, and the cockchafer as a symbol of fertility.

The Bushmen of southern Africa worship the praying mantis, which they believe is capable of speech. They have also invested it with supernatural status, believing it to be the creator of the moon and the protector of the antelope.

**Nature worship**
*The celebration of the natural world lingers on in modern times. At Pacific Grove in California a festival is held each year to celebrate the migration of the monarch butterfly.*

# CATS: GODS OR DEMONS?

*The sacred cat of ancient Egypt, extravagantly worshiped...the "witch's companion" of the Middle Ages, persecuted and tortured...the tiger, seen in the East as the personification of both good and evil — whether idolized or reviled, the cat has always exerted a powerful hold on man's imagination.*

*I*N PRE-CHRISTIAN TIMES the Egyptians worshiped the cat. In 80 B.C., in the ancient Egyptian city of Bubastis, the Greek historian Diodorus Siculus witnessed a striking demonstration of the cat's exalted status. As Diodorus recounted in his *Bibliotheca historica* (*Library of History*), a Roman soldier inadvertently killed a cat, and immediately a huge crowd, ignoring Egyptian officials' pleas for clemency, lynched the unfortunate man.

## Sun and moon

The Egyptians believed that the cat — probably first domesticated in Egypt sometime before 2500 B.C. — was the incarnation of Bast, goddess of the sun and moon, and a symbol of both fertility and virginity. The cat's association with the goddess may have been inspired by its eyes: by day golden, like the sun, by night reflecting light, like the moon.

## Great temple

The cult of Bast, which supplanted worship of the lioness-headed goddess of war, Sekmet, first became widespread in Egypt during the 10th century B.C., at the beginning of the 22nd dynasty. At Bubastis the Egyptians dedicated a great temple to Bast, approached by a broad avenue and almost surrounded by water. Visiting the city in the 5th century B.C., the Greek historian Herodotus marveled at the temple's magnificent central shrine. Hewn from red granite and encircled by trees, it contained an imposing stone statue of the cat-headed goddess, beneath which prowled the living sacred cats of her temple.

## Riotous festival

The annual springtime festival of Bast was the most popular in Egypt, and it is estimated that about three-quarters of a million people attended it, many traveling long distances to be there. More wine was drunk in Bubastis at this riotous festival, said Herodotus, than during the entire rest of the year. Most Egyptian homes contained a bronze statuette of Bast. This sometimes

The cat's association with the goddess Bast may have been inspired by its eyes: by day golden, like the sun, by night reflecting light, like the moon.

**Cat-headed goddess**
*This bronze statuette of the goddess Bast shows her with the customary four kittens at her feet.*

portrayed the goddess with cat's arms and legs, sometimes with human limbs; often she carried a shield, a basket, and a sistrum, a percussion instrument believed to have been used by women to ward off evil spirits.

### Shaved eyebrows

Living cats, as we have seen, were venerated also. Their owners pampered them and ornamented them with gold or silver earrings and chains and gem-studded collars. If a cat died naturally, everyone in the household would shave off his or her eyebrows as a sign of grief, hold a wake over the animal, and observe a period of mourning.

If a cat died accidentally in public, all those nearby would fall on their knees, declaring that they were not to blame. Yet, despite the gravity of the offense, the culprit might escape with his or her life; but if someone killed a cat deliberately, there was no reprieve — the offender was summarily executed.

### Demon-destroyers

After a cat died, Egyptians would embalm it, because they believed that in the next world cats were able to overcome demons and so protect the souls of the dead. After being embalmed, the cat's body was wrapped in linen, then sometimes sealed in a coffin of clay, wood, or bronze. It was then placed in one of the sacred cat cemeteries on the banks of the Nile.

### Cat mummies

These cemeteries often contained enormous quantities of cat mummies. In 1889 a necropolis at Beni Hasan, in central Egypt, was found to contain the remains of at least 300,000 cats, which together weighed some 19 tons.

An entrepreneur of the time devised a secular use for these sacred relics: crushed into powder, they might be used as a fertilizer. He exported them

to England for this purpose, and all that reportedly survives today of what was once an archeologically valuable collection is a single skull in the British Museum in London.

Not all unearthed feline mummies, however, have been destroyed like those of Beni Hasan. Many were preserved in museums. Some of these mummies are of domestic cats; others are of African wildcats. And in 1952 mammalogist T. C. S. Morrison-Scott announced that three skulls in a collection excavated in the early 1900's from tombs at Gizeh were of the jungle cat, which somewhat resembles the lynx in appearance.

### Devil's familiar

From Egypt the domestic cat spread to Asia and Europe, where it became a favored — though rare — pet of the Greeks and Romans. It did not become truly established in Western Europe until about 300 B.C., when it became mostly a valuable weapon against plagues of rats.

During the Middle Ages, however, the cat underwent a complete reversal in its status: from veneration in Egypt, as the reputed incarnation of a goddess, to persecution in Europe, as the alleged

**Bengali wood carving of a demonic cat**

familiar (or attendant spirit) of the devil. The cat's liking for darkness, its stealthiness in stalking its prey, its often withdrawn, inscrutable expression, the eerie glow of its eyes when reflecting light at night, the often bloodcurdling shrieks of males at mating time — all these combined to lead the more credulous in superstition-ridden medieval Europe to view the animal as a living embodiment of evil.

## Black cat idol

Because cats were seen as diabolic, people keeping them as pets were often hounded as witches or demon worshipers. From the late 13th to the

> During this period of oppression, cats were treated with great cruelty. In Metz, France, 13 cats were reportedly burned alive in hopes of halting an outbreak of the nervous disease Saint Vitus' dance.

early 18th century, cats — especially black ones — and their owners were frequently persecuted. In 1307 the Knights Templar (a religious order of knights who took part in the Crusades) were accused of worshiping a black cat idol, Baphomet, and kissing a cat during services. As a result Philip IV of France commanded the order to be suppressed.

## Burned alive

During this period of oppression, cats were treated with great cruelty. In Metz, France, 13 cats were reportedly burned alive in 1344 in hopes of halting an outbreak of the nervous disease Saint Vitus' dance (now known as Sydenham's chorea). And, to commemorate this bizarre episode, the practice was supposedly repeated annually until 1773.

The cat's supposedly sinister nature led to some strange beliefs. For centuries those living in the Scottish Highlands claimed that a species of strange creature lived there, one that they believed to be a witch in disguise. Calling the animal the *cait sith* (meaning "fairy cat"), they described it as a dog-size cat with spiky, white-flecked, black fur and a white throat.

Researchers considered the creature to be mythical, until 1983, when, at the village of Kellas in West Moray, Tomas Christie, a laird, shot a creature corresponding to those reputedly sighted over the centuries. Now known as the Kellas cat, it has been classified as a complex hybrid between the domestic cat and the Scottish wildcat. English zoologist Dr. Karl P. N. Shuker — who, in *Mystery Cats of the World* (1989), first drew attention to the similarity between the Kellas cat and the cait sith — has suggested that the two are one and the same creature, and that the cait sith can be added to the growing list of animals once thought mythical but now known to exist.

## Return to favor

Eventually, in the 18th century, the cat was restored to favor, and it became valued as a destroyer of brown rats, which were invading Europe from central Asia. Certain famed cat owners,

***Demon king***
*The cat appears in its diabolical role in this 19th-century engraving of the demon king Flauros from the French* Dictionnaire Infernal *(1864). Flauros is depicted with cat's head, tail, and claws.*

***Image of Satan***
*This illustration from a tract on witchcraft trials that took place in England in 1579 portrays a cat named Sathan (a variant of Satan) that figured in the trials. It invests the animal with the malevolence of its namesake.*

**Witch's alter ego?**
*This specimen of a Kellas cat, a hybrid between the domestic cat and the Scottish wildcat, was shot in 1983 in the Scottish Highlands. The Kellas cat is probably the basis for stories of the cait sith, the "fairy cat," which was once believed by Highlanders to be a transformed witch.*

such as the English man of letters, Samuel Johnson, helped to rehabilitate the animal. Famous owners in the 19th century included Abraham Lincoln and Charles Dickens. In 1871 a cat-lover in England named Harrison Weir organized the first cat show, and from then on the animal was well on its way to attaining the favored status it enjoys today.

It was not only the domestic cat that was worshiped in the distant past. Various wild cats were also regarded as sacred, among them the jaguar. As long ago as 1000 B.C. the Indians of Peru were carving images of jaguars on the pillars and walls of their highland temples. A few centuries later the Olmecs erected massive jaguar temples in Mexico. In these, jaguars are carved in the stonework, sometimes naturalistically but in other cases depicted as half-human. These creatures have been termed were-jaguars (from the Old English *wer*, meaning "man"). One, a figurine in the Dumbarton Oaks Collection in Washington, D.C., has eyes of pyrite (a brassy yellow metal), to make them gleam like those of real jaguars.

### Incarnation of the sun
The Tucano Indians of Amazonia venerated the jaguar as the incarnation of the sun, but the Mayas of

Mexico and Central America revered the animal as a terrifying symbol of the underworld and of earthly — as opposed to heavenly — forces. The Mayas used the jaguar's pelt, blood, claws, and teeth in their ceremonies and built numerous jaguar temples. One, in Tikal, Guatemala, still stands today, as does another, at Chichén Itzá, in Mexico, adorned by a jaguar-shaped throne.

According to Mayan belief, anyone who comes across a jaguar should not kill it but prostrate himself before it and await his fate. (In Bolivia, the Moxi tribe chose as its priests only those who had survived such confrontations with jaguars.) Jaguar worship survived in Mexico long after the decline of the Mayan civilization, until the 16th century, when the Spanish conquered the Aztecs.

### Jaguar medicine
In Paraguay, shamans (doctor-priests) of the now extinct tribe of Héta Indians had such faith in the magical properties of the jaguar that they would attempt to heal sick people by making them sit on a jaguar skin and waving another skin above them. Even today the cult of Nagualism, in certain remote areas of Central America, is partly based on the belief that a jaguar, or occasionally some other animal, acts as the familiar and guide of each member of the cult.

> **The Mayas revered the jaguar as a terrifying symbol of the underworld.**

### Puma shrine
Another wild cat that has been revered is the puma. The builders of Cuzco, Peru, constructed the city in the shape of a puma. In Sandoval County, New Mexico, a prehistoric puma shrine (the only one known in the United States) still exists. It bears a pair of sculpted pumas, carved by ancestors of today's Cochite Indians.

*Peruvian stone jaguar head, c. 1000 B.C.*

# IN THE FORESTS OF THE NIGHT

***The tiger inspires conflicting beliefs. Some primitive peoples see it as a beneficent being, while others associate it with evil spirits.***

*TYGER! TYGER! burning bright*
*In the forests of the night,*
*What immortal hand or eye*
*Could frame thy fearful symmetry?*

*In what distant deeps or skies*
*Burnt the fire of thine eyes?*

The opening lines of William Blake's famous poem "The Tyger" graphically epitomize the awe in which some have held this fearsome beast. In India some forest tribes worship it as a benevolent god and have built temples and shrines to it. In *The Book of Indian Animals* (1980), S. H. Prater, curator of the Bombay Natural History Society, describes how such people believe that they can protect tigers by deflecting bullets fired at them by hunters.

Yet in other parts of India the tiger has an evil reputation, based on more than its man-eating capability. Many tribes believe that the animal harbors the evil spirits of dead tyrants. Some African tribes have the same superstitious belief concerning lions.

## Yin and yang

In *Great Cats* (1991), biologist Dr. Susan Lumpkin, of the Washington Zoo, Washington, D. C., points out another conflict in religious attitudes toward the tiger: those of Taoism and Buddhism. In the first, the tiger represents yin (a dark, passive, female force, one of the two opposing powers controlling the universe), whereas in Buddhism the animal symbolizes yang (the light, active, male force). The complementary force in both religions is represented by the dragon.

**Protective headgear**
*In China, a child's headdress known as a tiger hat presents the animal as benevolent: It is believed to protect the wearer from harm.*

Another popular Indian belief concerning tigers, recorded in *The Book of Indian Animals,* is that if a man is killed by a tiger, his spirit will accompany that animal afterward to warn it of approaching danger. Sacred stones, painted red, are sometimes placed at sites where men have been killed by tigers, and it is said that if a person worships at one of these sites he will avoid meeting a similar fate.

## Secret city

Forest dwellers in Thailand and Malaysia believe that the tiger is the avenger of their supreme god and that it kills only those who have violated their sacred laws. Sumatrans once believed that tigers lived in a secret city deep in the heart of the jungle, a city that the animals had built from the bones, skin, and hair of human tiger-slayers.

Hindus have always viewed the tiger with awe and fear. In some regions of India, such as Purnia, the Hindus' terror of the animal was once so great that they referred to it only as *Janwar* (meaning "Beast") or by no name at all.

**On guard**
*A model tiger guards the entrance to a Buddhist retreat in Thailand. Buddhists believe that the animal symbolizes yang, the light, active, male force in the universe.*

# ANIMAL PANTHEON

*Various animals have been worshiped as the earthly representatives of gods, whose attributes these animals are believed to possess. Presented here is a further selection of deified creatures, including such unlikely objects of worship as the hippopotamus and the Pekingese dog.*

*Young aye-aye*

**Finger of death**
In Madagascar some villagers consider the aye-aye (a type of lemur) as sacred, and forbid anyone to harm it. But other Madagascans kill it on sight because they regard it as a harbinger of doom. They believe that if the animal points its strangely thin middle finger at anyone, that person will die.

*Australian Aboriginal paintings of kangaroos, on rock (above) and on bark (left)*

**Animal ancestors**
In Australia each Aboriginal tribe claims ancestors of a certain animal species, very often a marsupial (pouched mammal). There are kangaroo tribes, wallaby tribes, and so on. The belief in such man-animal kinship (also held by American Indians) is known as totemism.

*Egyptian statuette of a hippopotamus*

**Motherhood incarnate**
The hippopotamus seems an unlikely symbol of maternity, yet this was the role it played in ancient Egypt. The citizens of Thebes worshiped it as the incarnation of Taueret, goddess of both motherhood and destruction.

*Temple monkey, Nepal*

**Freedom of the temple**

In India monkeys are allowed to roam freely within temples, where they are regularly fed by both holy men and visitors.

*Carving of Ganesha, temple fragment*

**Guardians of paradise**

Among the most venerated animals of ancient China were lion dogs, the small, maned, pug-faced dogs that we know today as Pekingese. These animals were believed to guard the gates of paradise.

*Chinese ceramic lion dog*

**Symbol of success**

In India the elephant is the sacred symbol of the Hindu god Ganesha, who is regarded as a jovial deity. Always portrayed with an elephant's head and sometimes shown as riding a rat, Ganesha is the god of both knowledge and business success.

**Sumptuous seclusion**

Regarded by the Egyptians as the incarnation of Ptar, god of the arts, a sacred bull known as Apis was maintained in luxury and seclusion in a shrine at Memphis. When it died, it was embalmed, buried in a sarcophagus of pink granite, and replaced by another bull.

*Egyptian coffin painting of Apis*

# PHOTOGRAPHIC SOURCES

**Academy of Applied Science**/R.H. Rines, Boston, Mass. & Concord, N.H., 1972: 36-7, 40t; **Benedict Allen**: 74r; **Ancient Art and Architecture Collection**: 112tr, 120tr, 121tr; **Bodleian Library**: 98br, 99tr, 112tl, 113bl, 116t, 120bl; **Bridgeman Art Library**: 98tr, 99cl, 102t, 105b, 106t, 107, 108l, 112br, 117, 119tr, br, 120br; **British Film Institute**: 84-5 background, 97b; **British Library**: 111; **British Museum**: 29t, 95t, 140b, 141tr; Painted by **Zdenek Burian**, Prague: 31t; **Jean-Loup Charmet**: 112bl, 113tr; **Peter Clayton Associates**: 136l; **John Cleare/Mountain Camera**: 69r; **Bruce Coleman Ltd.**: 21cl (H. Reinhard), 24tr (O. Langrand), b (G. Cubitt), 34r (C.B. Frith), 35b (C.B. & D.W. Frith), 65b, 74l (L. Lee Rue), 75l, 86-7 (H. Reinhard), 103, 129 (A.J. Steven), 131br (M. Freeman), 133b, 139b (M. Freeman), 140tr (J. Cancalosi), 141tl (A.J. Deans); **Loren Coleman**: 68, 76r; **C.M. Dixon**: 21r, 127b, 128; **Essex Record Office**: 34l; **Mary Evans Picture Library**: 24tl, 50-1b, 54, 88b, 97t, 98tl, 106bl (from *The Arabian Nights*, illustrated by Edmund Dulac, reproduced by permission of Hodder & Stoughton Ltd.); **Werner Forman Archive**: 88tl, 95b, 116b, 132c, 140c; **Fortean Picture Library**: 20t (L. Coleman), b, 22 (J. Morris), 33r, 38b (A. Trottmann), 39, 40b (N. Witchell), 41, 121b (L. Thomas), 42l (M.P. Meaney), 48b, 51br, 58 (Patterson/Gimlin, copyright 1968 R. Dahinden), 59 & 60 (R. Dahinden), 64r, 89t, 138t (A. Barker); **Robert Harding Picture Library**: 132tl; **Bernard Heuvelmans**: 77l; **Michael Holford**: 82, 110t, 113tl, 141bl; **Hulton-Deutsch Collection**: 49t, 50t, cr, 51tl, 71br; **Hutchison Library**: 88tr, 105t (M. Macintyre); **The Image Bank**: 30 (Y. Kerban/Jacana); **Images Colour Library**: 50cl, 51tr, 94t, 106br, 113br, 118tr, c,

119bl, 124b, 126, 133t, 136r, 137, 139t, 141br; **International Society of Cryptozoology**: 55b; **Kinema Collection**: 84tr, b, 85t, bl, 90t, b, 91tl, b; **Kobal Collection**: 84tl, 85br, 90-1 background, 91tr; **Frank Lane Picture Agency**: 28b; **Dr. Roy P. Mackal**: 44b, 45b; **Simon Marsden Archive**: 80-1; **Missouri Historical Society**: 28t; **Colin Narbeth & Son Ltd.**: 83t; **Natural History Museum**, London: 32l, r (N. Parker), 76l, 77br; **Natural History Museum of Los Angeles County**/Photo by Richard Meier: 29b; **Natural History Photographic Agency**: 140tl (Silvestris); **Oxford Scientific Films**: 131tr (M. Fogden); **Pitt Rivers Museum**, Oxford: 93r, 94b; **Planet Earth Pictures**: 46-7 (P. David); **Popperfoto**: 96t; **St. Petersburg Times**, Fla.: 49b; **Science Photo Library**: 75r (J. Reader); Trustees of the **National Museums of Scotland**: 102b; **Dr. Myra Shackley**: 70c, 71bl; **South American Pictures**/M. & T. Morrison: 64tl, bl, 138b; **Frank Spooner Pictures**/Gamma: 42r (Liaison), 83b (A. Sassaki), 104, 124t (S. Basak), 127t (W. Stone), 130-1; **Survival Anglia**: 110b (D. & J. Bartlett); **David Towersey**: 96b, 99bl, 120tl; **UPI/Bettmann**, N.Y.: 26l; **Valley Morning Star**, Harlingen, Tex.: 31c; **Zefa**: 23 (Orion).

b - bottom; c - center; t - top;
r - right; l - left.

Efforts have been made to contact the holder of the copyright for each picture. In several cases these have been untraceable, for which we offer our apologies.